HERBERT CHAPMAN ON FOOTBALL

HERBERT CHAPMAN

on

FOOTBALL

THE REFLECTIONS OF ONE OF ARSENAL'S GREATEST MANAGERS.

First Published in Great Britain 1934 by Garrick Publishing Co.

This edition published 2011 by GCR Books Ltd.
Registered in England & Wales. Reg No. 6949535
www.gcrbooks.co.uk
ISBN 978-0-9559211-3-1

Photographs (pages 113-118) © Kenneth Chapman
Text and editing by GCR Books Ltd
Cover © Arsenal Football Club
Foreword © Greg Adams 2011

Printed and bound in Great Britain by CPI Mackays

FOREWORD

As a footballer, Herbert Chapman was nothing more than mediocre. He played mostly in the lower leagues, was never capped for his country and finished his full playing career with Tottenham Hotspur...which just about says all we need to know.

In 1907 he joined Northampton Town, one of his former clubs, as player manager. As a manager Chapman was a natural and a genius. He had great vision, innovative ideas in abundance, was head and shoulders above his counterparts and years ahead of his time.

Northampton was in the heart of rugby-loving England where football was very much the poor cousin. Northampton Town were languishing at the foot of the Southern League (League One in today's terms) having finished bottom two years running. He couldn't have started his managerial career with more of a challenge. However, Chapman was ambitious, introduced fresh ideas and adopted tactics that, along with a handful of big money signings, would bring almost instant success. The club finished eighth in Chapman's first full season and won the title the following year. They remained in the top four for the following three seasons before Chapman was tempted away by an offer from Leeds City (now Leeds United).

Chapman quickly turned around the fortunes of Leeds City finishing 6th and 4th in his first two seasons compared with 19th place and the need for re-election to the League before he arrived.

Unfortunately World War 1 was to interrupt his work and financial irregularities involving alleged illegal payments would result in the Club's expulsion from the Football League in 1918. Chapman unjustly received a lifetime ban which would later be overturned on appeal.

In February 1921 Chapman joined Huddersfield Town as assistant secretary-manager and was promptly promoted to secretary manager. In his first full season (1921-22) he guided the club to FA Cup success and 14th place in the league. Chapman strengthened his squad and the team finished third in 1922-23 before winning back-to-back titles in 1923-24 and 1924-25. He had his heart set on a third successive title but was lured away from Huddersfield in the close season.

Arsenal were seeking to replace their recently sacked manager and whilst the club were, in those days, nothing special, Chapman was attracted by the appeal of managing a London side, a bigger salary and the chance of weaving his magic on a larger stage. His Huddersfield team went on to complete their title hat-trick in his absence with Arsenal finishing second in Chapman's first season in charge. Aside from a Wembley FA Cup final in 1927, where the side lost 1-0 to Cardiff, there were few signs of progress. Chapman though remained optimistic and continued to build, mould and strengthen his squad. Success finally came in 1929-30 with Arsenal winning the F.A. Cup against Chapman's old club Huddersfield Town; their first major honour. The first League title came the following year with a record 66 points. The Club narrowly missed the League and Cup double a year later finishing runners-up in both competitions. League success was to follow again in 1932-33 and 1933-34.

Sadly, Herbert Chapman was not there to witness the back-to-back title triumph. Pneumonia brought his premature death on 6th January 1934, just 13 days before his 56th birthday. Arsenal Football Club, its fans and English football mourned his passing.

The Arsenal team that Chapman built went on to dominate English football throughout the 1930s winning five league titles and two FA Cups during this period. With Chapman's genius they had risen from virtual obscurity to become the greatest club in English football in less than ten years.

There may be some debate today as to whether Herbert Chapman is Arsenal's greatest ever manager; Arsene Wenger is undoubtedly a contender for this crown. However, what is certain is that Arsenal would not be where they are now were it not for the genius of this little man from Yorkshire.

This book, a collection of articles contributed by Herbert Chapman to *The Sunday Express*, sheds a little light on his career, his thoughts on football and his vision for the future of the game.

Greg Adams
gcrbooks.co.uk

"Herbert Chapman stands out today as quite simply the greatest visionary the English game has ever seen. His innovative ideas and forward-thinking nature propelled the game into the modern era and the unprecedented success he brought to Arsenal Football Club will never be forgotten."

Arsène Wenger

MR. HERBERT CHAPMAN'S ACHIEVEMENTS DURING HIS LAST TWELVE SEASONS AS A FOOTBALL MANAGER.

AT HUDDERSFIELD

1921-22. Huddersfield won the F.A. Cup
1923-24. Huddersfield won the League Championship.
1924-25. Huddersfield won the League Championship.

AT HIGHBURY

1925-26. Arsenal were runners-up to Huddersfield in the League Championship, obtaining a record number of points for a London Club.

1926-27. Arsenal were runners-up in the F.A. Cup.

1929-30. Arsenal won the F.A. Cup.

1930-31. Arsenal won the League Championship with 66 points, a record.

1931-32. Arsenal were runners-up both in the F.A. Cup and League Championship.

1932-33. Arsenal won the League Championship.

1933-34. At the time of Mr. Herbert Chapman's death on 6th January 1934 Arsenal were at the head of the League Table.

Arsenal Reserves won the London Combination
six years in succession.

CONTENTS

1

HOW I BECAME A FOOTBALL MANAGER

Most professionals who have won any distinction in the game hope that they remain in it when their playing days are at an end. Few, however, get the chance, and such men as Billy Walker, Jimmy Seed, and Tom Parker should count themselves lucky, even though it may not be long before the weight of responsibility which they have to bear makes them wonder whether they have chosen their new careers wisely. They are certainly sure to decide that it is easier to play than to manage.

When I arrived at the end of my playing career I had no intention of remaining in the game. I had been trained as a mining engineer, and I intended to go back to this work. What I believed was to be my last match for Tottenham Hotspur was against Brighton, and if I remember rightly I scored two goals from centre forward. I still recall my feelings as I lay in the bath after the match with Brighton. I decided that I had had a thoroughly good innings, and I had no regrets. It was goodbye to football and the start of a new life. But how curiously is one's life shaped. Before I left the

Tottenham dressing-room that afternoon I had made fresh plans.

We knew that it was also to be Walter Bull's last season at Tottenham. He had been appointed player-manager to Northampton, who were then at the bottom of the old Southern League. As I was dressing, Bull said to me, "I have decided to stay on another season with the Spurs, and you will have to take my place at Northampton." It may seem strange that two old players should presume to settle a matter of this sort between themselves, but, at any rate, it was in these circumstances that I went to Northampton and entered on a career which, because of its exacting character, allows one scarcely another interest.

Football had eaten deep into me and — well, my re-entry into mining engineering might be postponed for another year. But once at Northampton, and having become engrossed in the attempt to put the club on its feet, and encouraged by the feat of winning the old Southern League championship in the second season, I went on until I became permanently established as a manager.

When I went to Leeds City they were, like Northampton, at the bottom of the table. This was before the formation of the Third Division, and there was no system of relegation. The two bottom clubs, however, could only preserve their membership by re-election, and my first job was to visit all the clubs and appeal for their votes. The result was most encouraging, for we were re-elected with Lincoln City by a record number. In my second season at Leeds it seemed as if we might finish at the top of the Second Division. Our chief rivals were the Arsenal, but both of us were beaten at the post by Bradford and Notts County.

2

BUILDING THE TEAM

Team Selection — Practice Matches — Well-meant Advice — The Manager's Part — A Diagram of the Field — Players' Meetings — The Organisation of Victory — Soundness — Inviting Trouble — Watching Football — Slackness — An Example of Keenness — The Importance of Team-work — Danger of the Dominating Player — The Search for New Players — Brains — The Lack of Personalities — Holiday Matches — Demands of the Modern Game — The Ideal Team in Modern Football — A Team of Old Timers.

TEAM SELECTION

Not long ago I was discussing with some of my old Yorkshire friends the perplexing question of team selection. Should it be a one-man job, or should the full board of directors be responsible for it? I was told of one club in which, every Tuesday night, a dozen or so officials sit round a table and for two or three hours discuss the side to play on the following Saturday. That, to me, seems a ridiculous proceeding, especially having regard to what may happen in the meantime to affect the plans which may be made. Besides, you can never pick the best team in that way. It has been the way in which the international selectors choose the England side, and I have persistently condemned it on the ground that, when you have a dozen officials expressing their views as to the merits of players, without proper regard to blend and balance, the result cannot be satisfactory.

Team picking is a complicated and scientific matter requiring expert knowledge, and, in my experience, comparatively few directors are qualified to undertake it. I do not say this in any disparaging way. A director cannot have the same essential intimate knowledge of them men as those who live with them, and come to know and understand those peculiarities of temperament to which all of us are heir. My ideal selection committee is composed of three. This is how I would have the England team chosen, or, at any rate, I would have three members of the committee specially charged to nominate the players.

So far as clubs are concerned, in a good many cases they seem to be fettered by tradition. Thirty years ago all the directors joined in picking the team, and no-one today seems to be bold enough to suggest that the system is out of date and should be scrapped. In my opinion the club manager ought to pick the team. I would go further and say that he is the only official qualified to do so. If I were a director, I should take this view, and if a manager were not prepared to accept the responsibility, I should have no option but to decide that he was not worthy of his job.

"Thank goodness we've got a real manager at last, and I can now enjoy my football," a director of a leading club said to me one day, "I'm getting too old, or have lost my incentive to spend the weekends away from home looking for players, and I'm certainly very tired of being rung up and asked if Billy Jones can have a new pair of boots or if John Smith can have the weekend off. Our only grievance now is that we have nothing to do."

So much for the efficient manager. The truth is, football today is too big a job to be a director's hobby, and most clubs have recognised it, though I imagine in some cases authority has been surrendered to a paid official only with a good deal of reluctance. That is to be understood. There are some clubs, whose directors have had experience as players, who still carry on with the assistance of a secretary, and this may well be a proper course for them to adopt. The constitution of clubs varies considerably. In one you may have as many as thirteen directors, while in another only five. Some of us think that enough. Lucky the manager with a helpful board. Good boards make good managers. I agree that directors, with their authority and responsibility, should be kept fully informed on all matters relating to the team. They should be told of contemplated changes and the reason for them, and if the manager is trusted, there will never be any interference. It may be that suggestions will be offered, and if there is that frankness which should obtain, they will be carefully considered. But the decision should rest with the manager. How can a director, who never goes into the dressing-room, and perhaps would not be able to recognise a player off the field, fairly override him?

In all the positions I have held I have accepted the responsibility of choosing the team. It is not one, in my opinion, which can be shared. In every case, too, I have been loyally supported by my directors, and I recognise that this has largely contributed to any success I have achieved. I have always believed that a club should be like a big family, with all the members of it sticking and pulling together under one head.

PRACTICE MATCHES

What's the use of practice matches? I think the public are entitled to ask this question. They see the reserves beat the seniors, and when the team for the opening match is announced it comprises all the old players. In my view, the chief purposes the practice match serves are first that it is the best form of training, and then that it brings the men back to the realities of the game and fits them for the opening of the season.

But I have been too long in the game to be deceived by what these trials may seem to prove. I have never been associated with any club who have not been sure at the beginning of a season that they have found some bright young star who is going to stagger the football world by his brilliant achievements. Yet, in less than a month he is forgotten. Not only is there the danger of over-estimating the ability of a young or new player, because he is allowed more licence through his friendly opponents refusing to go the last yard against him, but one may go to the other extreme in judging the old players and decide that they are passing over the rickety bridge of age and are nearly finished.

WELL-MEANT ADVICE

I receive many letters during the season from supporters of the Arsenal suggesting ways and means by which the team might be improved. At least, they show a kindly interest in the fortunes of the club. One which arrived after four consecutive wins was startling. The proposal was that four of the players who had contributed to these successes should be dropped, and that their places should be taken by men from the reserves. The writer told me he lived in Felixstowe, and that he came every week to Highbury to see both the first and second teams. He was one of the regulars who took up their places in one of the corners of the ground, and after considering how the team might be improved, they asked him to put their conclusions before me. Why the changes should be made had been reasoned out, and I was told how better results might be achieved.

8

Drop four players! In all my experience of football management I cannot remember having made such sweeping changes to a side. I hate to have to make changes at all, and when they are necessary I try to arrange that they cause as little disturbance as possible. If I were to make four alterations in a team, unless they were due to circumstances over which I had no control, I should regard it as a confession that I had been seriously at fault previously in judging the merits of the men.

THE MANAGER'S PART

It is seldom that I miss a match. It is true that the work of finding new players must go on, but until a decision has to be made this is left to assistants. The scouting I do is chiefly in midweek, because I am convinced that it is more important that I should be with the team. Other managers take a different view, but they may not be so happily placed in the help they receive. If I were to go away, the Arsenal match policy would inevitably break down. I could not help to cure the faults of one game in preparation for another, if I had not seen the side play. I might try from what I had been told, but it is scarcely to be expected that the men would accept advice in those circumstances with the same readiness and confidence as if I had been present.

A manager may only work as circumstances will permit, but in my opinion, if he is to get the best out of the players, he must share their troubles, help them out of difficulties, and within the limits of discipline be their pal. Do you remember Carpentier and his inimitable manager, Descamps? They were truly a wonderful partnership: the understanding between the boxer and the little man with the black shining eyes in his corner was complete. I learned a good deal from the association of these two shrewd and quick-witted Frenchmen, who obviously had studied psychology most deeply, and by their understanding of human nature had formed an ideal partnership. Such a partnership may not be possible in football between a manager and his men, but to be successful they must always work together with confidence in each other and with the same common end in view.

A DIAGRAM OF THE FIELD

Some years ago I decided that it would be a good thing if players could be persuaded to give as much thought to the game as they did to their billiards and cards, which, instead of being a hobby, were almost a daily occupation. They were keen and ready enough to hold an "inquest" on the playing of a hand of solo, but they did not trouble to inquire why they had lost a match, or how the play of the side might be improved. At the time of which I write, most of the first class players came from Scotland and the north of England, and I found them extraordinarily shy and nervous. You would talk to them and they would say "Yes" to everything, but it did not follow they would carry out any promise you believed they had made. But they were ready enough to talk about football and tell you how this and that goal had been scored. As a manager I wanted to gain their confidence, and I realised that before I could do this it was necessary to dispel their nervousness. Only then could I hope that they would be frank. I conceived the idea of having a diagram of the field painted on the top of a table in my office, so that it would be in front of them when they came to see me. The scheme worked admirably, and at Leeds, Huddersfield, and the Arsenal I have found it to be of the greatest use. It has been a great help to me in explaining to a player some point of the game which I wished him to observe, and I am sure that to have the picture of the field before him has clarified the situation for him.

PLAYERS' MEETINGS

I also found that, having broken the ice, as it were, players at private interviews could be encouraged to express their own views, and occasionally to suggest how a colleague might play a more helpful part in the team. So I thought it

11

would be a good idea if I got the men together each week before a match to discuss the good and the poor points of the play of the previous week. My first experiment in this was at Leeds. Each Saturday morning, when we were at home, the men were instructed to attend one of the hotels in the centre of the city. A light lunch was followed by a talk among ourselves, and the home record of the team proved that the arrangement was an admirable one.

I have since adopted it on every occasion, both for home and away games. I preside at these meetings, and although in the frank discussion a player may feel a little hurt in being singled out for some fault in the previous week's game, a little tact and good humour quickly remove this. It is no use for a manager of whoever is in charge of the meeting to do all the talking, with the players mutely listening, and perhaps deciding that all that may be said is a lot of bunkum. Every man should be encouraged to talk and express his views without a fear that he will hurt any one's feelings. I have known complaints to be made because a man has "slanged" a colleague on the field, but in my time it was not unusual for players to criticise each other. In discussing this point Alex James once said that the old Celtic teams always seemed to be having a row amongst themselves, and that the harder they went for each other the better they played.

I am convinced that much of the success achieved by the Arsenal has been through the team quickly sensing a weakness in the opposition. Indeed, this has been a very remarkable feature of our displays, and I assure you that this is not an accident. We know our opponents before we take the field, or believe we do, and in our discussions on the match, in which every man speaks frankly, without a fear of hurting any one's feelings, the last detail of the plan by which we hope to win is studied. We are prepared, and though the plan may go wrong, it does not follow that it has been ill-conceived. Moreover, it may be altered at half-time. I freely confess that these match talks have been of inestimable value to me. I have learned much from them. They have given me new ideas, which I have put into practice. I am always looking for new ideas. I would borrow one from a programme boy at Highbury, if it were a good one.

THE ORGANISATION OF VICTORY

In my playing days no attempt was made shall we say, to organise victory. The most that I remember was an occasional chat between, say, two men playing together on a wing with a view to arriving at an understanding. Later, trainers tried to encourage friendship. Another development of the idea was made by the England selectors. For very good reasons they had come to fear Alan Morton, and in the international match of 1925 with Scotland they adopted a plan which they hoped would stop the havoc which the "Little Blue Devil" regularly caused. It was entirely mistaken, as they were to discover, and it never had a chance of succeeding.

Because Magee in the West Bromwich Albion team was in the habit of marking the outside forward, they selected him with the intention that he should shadow Morton. Whether Magee was told of the special duty he was expected to undertake I do not know, but the position was a hopeless one for him. The tactics of one man never won a match, and unless the other members of the side work in conjunction with him, he will probably lose it. What happened was so elementary that it should have been foreseen. It was only necessary for the Scottish inside-left to hold the ball, to compel Magee to move inside to tackle him, and before he could do this the ball was slipped out to Morton, who was left to go on without a challenger. As a bit of secret history in connection with this match, I may say that an old Scottish player resident in London wrote to the Scottish captain and told him what the English plan was, and also how it might easily be beaten.

The day of haphazard football, when men went out to do their bit according to their own ideas has gone. All teams are now highly organised, and players, I am sure, do not like to be left to their own resources. The cleverest men in the game welcome a settled policy. In fact they expect it, knowing that it is going to make the game very much easier for them. If the clubs believe that plans are necessary for a match, it is surely even more important in the case of a scratch side, and until the authorities are prepared to be modern enough to study the art of winning, English international football will never be as good as it might be. England should not lose even to Scotland, and I do not believe they would, if the matches were tackled with the same keenness and thoroughness as a League club are compelled to bestow on all their games.

SOUNDNESS

I do not know whether it is appreciated, but the Arsenal's preparations for London Combination matches are just as thorough as those for League games. If the plans are good for one team, they are good for the other, and, besides I take the view that all the players of a club should be trained along the same lines. In what other way can youths be developed for promotion? When one is brought into the senior side, it is expected that he will as nearly as possible produce the same game as the man who has fallen out would have done. Only in that way can the team-work be preserved. In the circumstances, it follows that he must be brought up to practise the recognised methods of the club.

I do not wish it to be assumed that our object is to make all Arsenal players bear the imprint of the same mould. That would be foolish in the sense that it would stifle individuality and prevent a youth developing so as to make the most of his natural talents. It is not true that Arsenal players are slaves to a system. The fact that their game is never stereotyped proves this. But there are fundamental principles as to methods and teamwork which we believe must be observed, and to this extent I admit that the men are expected to play to plan. I will go further and say that if they never departed from it we should lose fewer matches.

The keynote of Arsenal football is soundness. It is only when the team are, say, two goals up that they may claim the licence to be spectacular. From this point of view I am beginning to wonder whether adequate credit is given to defence. Football, at least in these days, is just as much a matter of saving goals as scoring them, and there is as much art and skill in one phase of the game as there is in the other. In my view, it is impossible in any team game to divorce defence from attack. One is as important as the other. It is undoubtedly true that a victory can often be traced back to the soundness of the defence. Those whose duty it has been to hold up the opposition until a scoring opening could be found have played a greater part than the forwards who have contrived to get the ball into the net. Unfortunately, defence does not make the same popular appeal. There is seldom any thrill in a tackle, and if a back should head the ball out from under the bar, all the sympathy is with the side who have, fortuitously, as it may seem, been robbed of a goal. All the glamour of the game, the be-all and end-all in the eyes of so many, is in seeing the ball pass into the net, and it does not matter a great deal how it arrives there.

Defence has been perfected to a remarkable degree, and I have heard it suggested that through its further development football may be brought to a state of stalemate. That was never the position under the old offside law, and it will be a sorry reflection on forwards if they have not the intelligence, the inventiveness, to devise means by which they can carry their attacks to a successful end.

INVITING TROUBLE

Experience has taught us in the League that it is never safe to regard a match as won until it is at an end, and any team who depart from the methods which have given them their advantage are inviting trouble. Almost the only time when risks in defence may be justified is when it is a question of making up goals which have been lost. Only then would I approve of a centre-half going up to force the attack. I would also stress the fact that no match in these days can be counted easy to win. Should it happen to be won easily, it is an accident.

WATCHING FOOTBALL

I am convinced that it is good for the player sometimes to look on, for there is much to be learned from the stand. But, as I have told many young players, they should not sit and eat sweets or smoke a chain of cigarettes. They ought not to regard it as their holiday. Football is their job, and it is up to them to seize every opportunity to improve their knowledge and understanding on the game. They can only do this provided they are prepared to pay attention to all the details which perhaps mean little to the ordinary spectator. For a young footballer to assume the nonchalant attitude towards a match is a misuse of a fine opportunity, and the players of the Arsenal who are allowed to look on know that a good deal more is expected from them. Indeed, they realise that at the meeting the following week they will be asked to express the views they have formed in regard to pertinent features of the play, and to offer reasons why the game was won or lost.

The Arsenal Club have always encouraged boys to watch the matches at Highbury. They will be the men of tomorrow, and we hope they will become regular supporters. But we do not wish to take them from their own games. They are better playing than looking on, and I know that many of those who pass through the turnstile specially provided for them have had their matches in the morning.

One day, shortly before the start of a match with Middlesbrough, I received a telephone call from the Rev. R. G. Hunt, who told me that he would like to bring forty boys from Highgate School, and I was delighted to do what I could at such short notice to find them accommodation. Mr. Hunt explained that under normal conditions the boys would have been playing themselves, but as the ground was unfit, it was a good opportunity for them to see a first-class match. "I am a great believer in youngsters watching really good players," he said. "They can learn a great deal."

In a letter I received from him afterwards he said he was delighted to see how both sets of forwards kept the ball on the ground. He added, "I see very little football now, and from what I have been told I gathered that post-war football had deteriorated. After your match with Middlesbrough I do not agree."

I highly value this opinion. Mr. Hunt was a member of the Wolverhampton Wanderers team who beat Newcastle United in the Cup Final of 1908, and he has also played against Scotland. Obviously, he is very well able to judge and to compare the football of today with that of twenty years ago, and it is pleasing to have his favourable opinion.

Mr. Hunt is undoubtedly right in saying that the young player can learn by watching. I remember once being in Scotland and having a youth pointed out to me. It is some years ago, and I cannot recall his name, but I was told that he was regarded as the understudy of that wonderful inside-forward of the Celtic, McMenemy, and that it was considered more important that he should sit in the stand and study the latter's style than that he should always play in the reserve side.

SLACKNESS

I will never tolerate slackness. If it enters a team, there can be no success that is worthwhile. That, at any rate, is my view, and frankly I cannot be bothered with any man unless he is prepared to give his whole mind to his job. His job, too, does not consist simply in paying attention to his own particular part. He has other interests besides his own. He is one of eleven men forming a team, and no matter where the ball may be, his mind should never be off it. Sometimes, when the ball is on the opposite side of the field, you see a wing forward lounging about with his hands in his pockets, as it were, his mind obviously vacant to matters which may very soon demand his fullest attention. He makes no attempt to anticipate the next move. Such players—and there are, I regret, many in football at the present time—should be made to take a course of mental training. If they are ever to make good as satisfactory team men, pulling their full weight throughout the ninety minutes, they ought to learn that they must never be off their toes, and must watch eagerly for a chance to come in and help their side.

AN EXAMPLE OF KEENNESS

When Alex James was taken to the dressing-room during the Arsenal's opening match with Birmingham in the autumn of 1933, he was in great pain. His ankle had been very badly hurt, and I was anxious that he should go to hospital at once. He declined, however, insisting on being allowed to stay until the game was over.

When the players came off the field at half-time, he was lying on a table still suffering acutely, but it was evident that his thoughts were still on the match, and he called to me and suggested the adoption of tactics which he believed might make up for his absence from the field, and possibly lead to the scoring of one or more goals. The players went out, and shortly afterwards he heard the muffled sound of cheering, and he insisted on knowing what had happened. When he was told that Jack had scored, he raised his head from the table and clapped his hands, telling how deep was his interest in the Arsenal team, even when in so much pain.

THE IMPORTANCE OF TEAMWORK

A player's value should be judged on his ability to fit in with the other members of the team. The best player who ever kicked a ball would be small use if he were as one apart. This is the danger of every transfer. No player can be worth his price unless he becomes a team man. May I draw on Alex James to emphasise the truth? He has always been a wonderful individualist. In Lancashire it was said that Preston North End comprised James and ten others. The statement was also put into the mouth of James that in no circumstances was he ever going to chase an opponent in possession of the ball. James possibly held something like this view when he arrived at Arsenal, and it probably accounted for the idea that he would never be any use to the team. But his mind was big enough to allow him to sink much of his individuality in his play, in order to fit in with the schemes of the team. I know that many old players advised him that he had made a mistake, and it was declared that his play at the end of the season had deteriorated. This was not the view of the Arsenal, and I should be very surprised if it was the opinion of James. All the time he has been in London his value has continued to increase.

DANGER OF THE DOMINATING PLAYER

A club is naturally glad when it discovers a star player, but there is a danger in allowing him to dominate a team, owing to the difficulty of filling his place. This may be pointed to in many cases. The retirement of Joe McCall, perhaps the best centre half of his type since the War, marked the decline of Preston North End as a senior club. Sheffield Wednesday have never been the same since Jimmy Seed left, and they say at Hillsborough today that their troubles would pass in a night if he could only come back to lead the team. So greatly were Tottenham Hotspur dependent on Arthur Grimsdell as the "father" of the side, that his loss was irreparable. When he dropped out, the club went into the Second Division. It is perhaps an exaggeration to attribute all the misfortunes of the club to this cause, but as the best left half of his day, and one of the greatest of all times, Grimsdell was an enormous factor in their success. Clem Stephenson at Huddersfield and now Billy Walker at Aston Villa are other key players who have caused much trouble in the rebuilding of their sides. At Huddersfield Stephenson has had the severe task of making good his own loss, and I warmly congratulate him on the judgment he has shown not only in filling the gap which he caused himself, but the others which have occurred.

No club has been more successful than Aston Villa through all the years in maintaining the high standard of the team. Their secret lies in always looking ahead and in patiently allowing their players to develop according to their needs. They have never hesitated to pay for the player they believed they required, and the policy has been abundantly justified. My experience has convinced me that there is one golden rule which must be obeyed. It is never safe to be satisfied. No matter how good the team may be, there should always be an attempt to improve it. A team may run smoothly and evenly for a year or so, and there may be no suspicions of any weakening, but unless there is progress, there is, in my opinion, bound to be decline, and I think that many of the troubles clubs experience can be traced to the fact that they are content to maintain a good team without trying to back it up and strengthen it in the Aston Villa way.

THE SEARCH FOR NEW PLAYERS

The search for men is being carried on energetically. Every week club representatives are engaged in trying to find players. But there is nothing unusual in this. It is their job, and it does not follow that they have any immediate purpose. Every Monday morning I receive the reports of the Arsenal scouts, and the information is often valuable, even if it is of a negative character. This work is carried out in order to provide for the emergency which may arise at any time. If a player should suddenly be needed, I do not want to be in the position of wondering where he can be found. To begin the search then means a waste of time, and under the system we have adopted we are kept in the closest touch with the game and the players.

Because a club representative visits a match, it does not follow that he has any instructions to act or even to inquire as to the possibilities of a transfer being arranged. Scouts will tell you that not once in a dozen matches do they come across a player whom they can confidently recommend. The most familiar report I receive is: "Not good enough for you." There are hundreds of men looking for players every Saturday, yet the number of those who cause "negotiations" to be opened is astonishingly small.

BRAINS

I am always sorry for clubs who have to act hurriedly in seeking a new player, for under the most favourable conditions it is tricky business and demands the closest consideration. It is not enough that a man should be a good player. There are all sorts of other important factors to be taken into account. This takes time. The longer I have been on the managerial side of the game, the more I am convinced that all-round intelligence is one of the highest qualifications of the footballer. I suppose one of the best teams there has ever been was that claimed by Newcastle United for ten years or so before the War, and the part which so many of them have since played in the game indicates that they were intellectually above the average.

We at the Arsenal have been similarly fortunate in our choice of players, notably in Buchan, Parker, Jack, James, Coleman, and Hulme, and I attribute much of the success we have achieved to the fact that our men had the good sense to realise that their own destiny as well as that of the club rested with themselves. Brains and the general character of players are more important today than they have ever been.

THE LACK OF PERSONALITIES

Football today lacks the personalities of twenty or thirty years ago. This, I think, is true of all games, and the reason for it is a fine psychological study. The life which we live is so different: the pace, the excitement, and the sensation which we crave are new factors which have had a disturbing influence. They have upset the old balance mentally as well as physically, and they have made football different to play as well as to watch. And they have set up new values. The change has, in fact, been so violent that I do not think the past, the players and the game, can fairly be compared with the present.

It is sometimes said that, if the old players were to come back, they would show up the limitations of the men of today. But there is no coming back. I know how boldly and confidently the old-timers speak of their prowess, and how they are inclined to belittle present-day players. To support their arguments, they point to the difficulty of the selectors in trying to build up a stable international side. England teams come and go. From one season to another they can scarcely be recognised. They have, unfortunately, to be altered from match to match. Men good one day fail the next. They do not even play consistently in their club form. This is one tell-tale piece of evidence of how football has changed. In the old days the right of six or seven men to be picked was not questioned, and they never let the side down. Because of this, team selection was a comparatively easy matter.

I am not prepared to depreciate the men of today, being fully conscious of the many matters which have added to their difficulties. Competition has been heightened enormously, and it is no longer possible for men or teams to play as they like. Thirty years ago men went out with the fullest licence to display their arts and crafts. Today they have to make their contribution to a system. Individuality has had to be subordinated to teamwork. Players have to take part in many more matches, and the strain on their physical resources has greatly increased. The strain, too, has been intensified by the demands of the public. This is a point which I am afraid is only slightly appreciated.

HOLIDAY MATCHES

My attention has often been drawn to the large number of injuries which are sustained during the Christmas fortnight, and I have been asked to explain them. In the first place, it should be realised that during this short period some teams have to play six matches, which is ordinarily equivalent to six weeks' football. Men too, are absent from teams not because they are seriously hurt, but simply because there is not sufficient time to cure their bruises and sprains. In ordinary circumstances we should not have heard of them. In the usual interval between one match and the next they would have been successfully treated by the trainers.

It has been suggested that footballers who spend their whole time keeping fit should have no difficulty in playing four matches in eight days, but even in my playing days it was a task from which one would have been glad to be relieved, and today, with the pace of the game so greatly accelerated, it is considerably harder. I agree that the trouble is chiefly with men bordering on the thirties and over. In their case, muscles have lost some of their elasticity, and they take longer to recover from the effects of a keen match. One of the most famous players of his time told me that during his last seasons he never made a complete recovery after a Saturday match until the following Wednesday, and it is undoubtedly true that when a man passes the age of thirty he finds two games a week a sore trial.

Much, too, depends on the state of the ground on which he plays. A heavy one adds to the strain. Again, the long journeys which a player has to undertake are tiring. This is not only true from a physical point of view: he also loses some of his zest for the game. He is not in a fit state mentally to fight with his customary enthusiasm, and without enthusiasm he is merely an imitation of himself. He is willing enough, and he goes out with the intention of doing his utmost, but as the strain tells, he is very much inclined to weaken morally. It is no longer only necessary for a team to play well. They must get the goals, no matter how, and the points. The measure of their skill is, in fact, judged by their position in the league table, and they have to bend all their efforts to ensure that this is a good one.

DEMANDS OF THE MODERN GAME

Even if the modern game be not harder, it is very much more exciting. This has come about swiftly since the alteration of the off-side law. The object of this was largely to reduce the number of stoppages and to please the onlooker, but I sometimes wonder whether it would have been made if it had been realised how the structure of the game as well as the players was to be changed. Clubs would, I think, have pondered long over it if it could have been foreseen how managerial difficulties were to be increased. Having been educated on different lines, I doubt very much whether the public would today be satisfied with the old football, with all its precision and deliberate accuracy. It does not fit modern tendencies. It would be out of tune with the bustle and excitement of everyday life. Spectators want a fast-moving spectacle, rapier-like attacks that have the spirit of adventure, and ever more goals. The heavier the scoring, the more appealing is the match.

But I should do an injustice to the old-timers if I did not believe that they would have been able to accommodate themselves to modern requirements. Their natural ability would have ensured this, but they would have had to alter their whole mode of life. They would find that the game now carries far greater responsibilities than they used to bear, and they would have to tackle it far more thoroughly, and, to succeed, make many personal and social sacrifices. They would discover, too, that the play made greater demands on them. They would have to keep much fitter; otherwise, instead of being "ninety-minute men," they would fade out very quickly. No one can amble through a game today, taking rests when the need is felt, and there can be no abuses of training without the penalty being paid. The modern pace would kill the old footballer in a month, unless he were prepared to adapt himself to the conditions. He would also have to change his methods, to suit the systematised style of play.

I have been told that there is too much system, and that those of us who are said to have conspired to bring it about have been responsible for driving out the individual touch. The truth is that the exigencies of the game have left us no alternative. We have been compelled to scheme, to produce the results which the public demand.

But, while admitting this, I do not believe that the game when played well under modern conditions has lost its attractiveness. The changes which have come about have brought excellent new features. It is true that the dribble has largely disappeared. In its place is the twenty-yard pass, which has a faster purpose, and is probably even more effective. I think it will be conceded that the clubs are good judges of the type of play which satisfies the public taste. Can it be believed that the Arsenal, in order simply to produce results, would cultivate a style that did not appeal to the fans?

THE IDEAL TEAM IN MODERN FOOTBALL

(Herbert Chapman selected this ideal team in February 1931)

I sometimes wonder what an ideal team would be like according to modern conditions. Suppose all the players one might wish to select were available, of what type would they be? If I were looking for a goalkeeper, I do not think I could find one more suitable than a quick and daring Rugby fullback, who could kick strongly with both feet and catch a ball with the certainty of a fielder in the slips. He would also require to be tall, somewhere about six feet, so that when the ball came over from the wings he would be able to punch it out, and by the use of his hands beat the Hodgsons and Deans with their heads.

The game today demands that a back should be speedy, quick in turning, so that he may go back to recover, and clever enough in ball play to be able to work his way out of a tight corner. A player who is well equipped with these qualifications is Blenkinsop of the Wednesday. Another notable feature marks his play. He has the very valuable knack of keeping the man and the ball in front of him. You do not see Blenkinsop rush recklessly into a tackle. The clever forward likes an impetuous defender, because he is so easily sidestepped and beaten. The back a forward does not relish is one who stands off and compels him to take the ball up.

The centre half should act mainly on the defensive and become largely a third back. Personally, I like a tall man as centre half, and one of his qualifications is that he should be good with his head, owing to the fact that the ball so often goes to him in the air. This is, of course, specially the case in regard to goal kicks. If he is accomplished in the use of the ball, pushing it through down the middle or sending it out to the wings, so much the better; but if he does not excel in this phase of the game, I think the trouble can be overcome, provided there is the right blend of wing halves. For a wing half I like a player who has had experience as a forward. For example, a Strange or a Charlie Jones, because they have such good understanding of what is required to support an attack. Having been in the positions themselves, they realise how a forward likes to receive the ball, and how they can help by positional manoeuvring.

It used to be thought that the centre half was the key man of a team. Today, I think, there are four key men – the two wing halves and the two inside forwards. The centre half may still play an important part in a constructive sense, but under the altered conditions the wing men have more scope as schemers, and it is on this account that such players as Strange, Bob John, Campbell, and Jimmy McMullan are so valuable. If I had a boy whom I wanted to make a wing half I would say, "Go and study McMullan's play. He is the model of all I can conceive in correctness."

Coming to the forwards, we find a notable change in the play of the wing men. In their case, pace is more than ever important. They should make ground quickly, and now that the danger of being jockeyed into off-side positions is less, they have far greater opportunities than the old players possessed. Their duties, too, have changed, in the sense that, whereas it used to be thought that their main job was to get the ball across to make chances for the insides, they now have exceptional scoring opportunities themselves. But they must break away from the old idea that their place is on the line. They should always be ready to move inside, not only when they have the ball themselves, but whenever there is a likelihood of it coming over from the opposite wing. In these circumstances it follows that they should, as we say, have two feet, and be able to shoot like a Hooper with both. Another wing player who has been quick to grasp his scoring opportunities is Davis of Bradford.

Give me a Strange and a McMullan in the wing half positions, Jack and James as the inside forwards, and a Dean as the centre, and I should think I was getting very near to my ideal. Add two fast scoring outside players, and the plan would be as complete as I could ever expect to make it.

A TEAM OF OLD-TIMERS

In an idle moment I set down this team of old players, to amuse myself in comparing them with the chief players of today:

Hardy;
Crompton, Pennington;
Warren, Roberts, Needham;
Simpson, Bloomer, Shepherd, Holley, Spikesley

This is truly a wonderful array of the richest talent, and it goes a long way to convince one that football has lost its personalities. Some of these men have, in my judgement, never been equalled. The game has produced no goalkeeper so sound and safe as Sam Hardy; I have never known a back with such giant qualities as Bob Crompton, and Jesse Pennington with his magnificent enthusiasm and speed in recovery was the ideal partner. Modern half-backs, too, fail in comparison with poor Ben Warren, a human steam-engine, who played through ninety minutes with intimidating strength and speed. Roberts was contemporary with Wedlock, and it was the latter who gained the international honours, but I have always suspected that it was the outspokenness of the Manchester United captain which caused him to be passed over in the selection of England's team. I shall always think that Needham was the finest footballer I have ever seen. He was my hero as a boy, and I shall never forget how he seemed to attract the ball as if it were a magnet.

There have been outside rights who have shown more artistry than Simpson, who played so much of his football in Scotland before joining Blackburn Rovers, but he was unique in many respects. The way in which he got the ball over when he did not appear to have a chance was wonderful, and he was one of the first players to show that men in his position on the wing might play a considerable part in the scoring. Bloomer was the match winner, but in his case I fear that if he had had to do all the chasing of the modern inside forward he would have been less successful. Albert Shepherd could have stepped out of the old into the new football with little trouble. Indeed, he practised much the same style as the centre forwards of today, waiting for the ball to be put through to him so as to go between the backs and shoot. George Holley was another great inside forward; in the opinion of Charlie Buchan, the most complete one during that pre-war golden era; and Fred Spikesley, in my judgment, was unsurpassed in poise and balance and ability to work the ball with both the inside and outside of the feet – both feet.

I am afraid it inevitably seems that we have now few of such giants, but they would have different values today. They would have to be content with less individual greatness and strive for more uniformity than was considered necessary in their time. And it will perhaps be thought that I have not answered the question – were the old players better than the new? There is no answer. The way in which the game has changed forbids any comparison.

3

THE TRANSFER MARKET

Some Leading Questions — "Difficult" Players — The
Management Committee — Protection of the Clubs — A
Player's Obligations — The Transfer List — The Wage
Problem — Transfer Prices — Scottish and English Football
Compared — Making Enquiries — Signing on the Stars —
My First Attempt to Sign on Dunne — How I Won a Cigar —
The Art of Salesmanship — Disappointments — The £10,000
Fee.

SOME LEADING QUESTIONS

Is the buying of players fair? Does the
system give rich clubs an unfair advantage? Would
it be better if the game were less commercialised?
Should players have to acquire a residential
qualification?

First, as to its fairness from the point of
view of the player. About five years ago the
Birmingham Club invited the Arsenal to transfer
Lambert, and owing to the fact that we had plenty
of forwards at the time, we were prepared to
consider an offer. The player was consulted, and he
said, "I like being with the Arsenal, and I don't
think there is a better club. I'm not going to leave."
This immediately brought the negotiations to an
end. The player is always master of his own

destiny. He has his contract, and no club can break it by forcing him to go to another. There can never be a transfer unless the player approves of it. Obviously, too, it is often in the interests of a player to change his club, for it probably means giving him greater opportunities. In one he is a reserve, and in the other, he jumps straight into the first team. By moving he may also benefit financially. It is not every club which can afford to grant benefits, and at the end of five years there is never any guarantee that a man will receive the reward he hopes for. But if he is transferred, the position is entirely different. Then it is the general practice to allow him a sum in lieu of the benefit he might or might not have received, had he remained for five years or more.

In regard to the fairness of the system from the point of view of the clubs, I would point out that they neither buy nor sell a player unless it is to their advantage, and that whatever money changes hands is put into circulation in the game. This must always be so as long as it is a rule that no higher dividends than 7.5 per cent can be paid. As a matter of fact, there are clubs who could not live without the transfer system. It is only by obtaining money for players that they can pay their way, and yet in some cases they squeal and declare that they have not a chance with what they are pleased to call their rich rivals. Take the case of directors who have an overdraft at the bank, and who are pressed to clear it off or reduce it. They immediately look around and say, "Have we got a player whom we can spare and realise on?" At such anxious times it is the transfer system which comes to their rescue.

In dealing with the second question, whether the system gives the rich clubs an advantage, I would cite Tottenham Hotspur as the best answer. They are rich beyond doubt, but their position was not built up through the transfer system. As a fact, I know that during the years Peter McWilliam was there, they were outstanding as good sellers, and that they received more from the disposal of players than they paid for new ones.

It is still a question of outlook and enterprise, to which the third query, as to the way in which the game is commercialised, is related. We may not like it, but football from the point of management is largely a business on a very considerable scale, and the clubs may be compared to the big stores and the small shops on opposite sides of the street. One side dresses its windows most attractively to invite trade, and the other, less ambitious and venturesome, is content to jog along in a much more modest way. I agree that the opportunities are not the same. The club in a small town has not the same scope for expansion as one in a big populous centre, but both are in the game in the hope that they may get the most out of it for the good of the game and their supporters, and must be allowed to develop according to their plans and possibilities.

But though the conditions vary considerably, it surely cannot be suggested that all should move at the same pace. I am convinced, too, that many clubs do not make the most of their chances. Well do I remember the position at Huddersfield in their early days. They used almost to count the spectators in hundreds, and, owing to the competition of Rugby, they were told that they had no chance. But the new directors took a different view, and, by their daring and enterprise in getting together a first-class team, won over the people to what was to them a new game.

Now, finally, as to the question of residential qualification. It is good to see local players in a team, but the view I take is that football today is a world's entertainment, and that it is my responsibility, as the showman I am supposed to be, to put on the best possible programme. Indeed, the game as it is has grown and developed demands this, and I must look for my players, my stars, wherever they are to be obtained.

"DIFFICULT" PLAYERS

No man in this hard work-a-day world receives more consideration than the professional footballer, and because of the shortness of his career, and the perilous risks he is bound to run, he is shown kindness and sympathy. I believe that men who are ambitious and keen to make the best of their abundant opportunities appreciate their good fortune. They are truly well off as compared with the players of even twenty years ago. But, as is inevitable in so large a community, there are the malcontents – men who seem to seek grievances and have many grumbles. There are, unfortunately, too, those who, perhaps because of the indolent lives they are ready to live, refuse to observe the code of discipline which must be observed in every club, and make themselves an intolerable nuisance. They are few, but, because of their conduct, I fear they may create a false impression in the public mind.

It is unfortunate, but I think it will be appreciated that it is very necessary, that there should be rules and regulations to deal with these "difficult" players. In these circumstances it may happen that a well-behaved player has to suffer, and I fear it is on this account that complaints are made against the transfer system.

THE MANAGEMENT COMMITTEE

It must not be thought that Mr. John McKenna and his fellow-members of the management committee would knowingly allow a man to be unfairly treated. The player has always a right of appeal to them, and, provided he has a good case, he is certain to win their sympathy. I could tell of many instances in which Mr.

McKenna has personally appealed to clubs to alter their decisions in favour of players when perhaps the facts did not wholly justify contrary action. The footballer has no better friend than Mr. McKenna, and there could be no bigger mistake than to regard his as the representative of the clubs. In the 1931-32 season, when drastic steps were taken to economise, it was suggested that there should be a cut in players' wages. "I will not agree to that", he said, in his emphatic and downright way. "I do not believe it is necessary." It should be realised too that the management committee know of most of the things that take part in the game.

It is said that the transfer system is "un-English." Well, there is nothing "un-English" about the management committee.

PROTECTION OF THE CLUBS

In judging the justice of the transfer regulations, it should first be realised that professionalism could not be controlled, and that the clubs would be brought to a state of chaos, without them. There have been complaints against the system almost as long as it has been in operation, but no one has ever been able to suggest an alternative one. If transfers were abolished during the season, it would only mean that there would be an end to the movement of players from one club to another. Such an embargo would not only be ridiculous, but grossly unfair to both player and club. I think it will also be realised that players cannot be permitted to come and go at will. Clubs must have some protection, not only so far as the players they pay for are concerned but for those whom they engage as youths and train themselves, for they, too, may be found costly when the amount they draw in wages before they mature and become good enough for the League side is taken into consideration.

Clubs must have some hold over their players, otherwise they could not commit themselves to such great financial responsibilities. How could grounds worth £100,000, or more, be maintained if, at the end of a season, they were to be the victims of the caprice of the players, and teams were liable to be broken up? Such a possibility is too absurd even to contemplate. Directors who provide the ground, and guarantee the wages of the club staff for a year, must never be allowed to be the victims of the unscrupulous player who is a party to a transfer arrangement which has been to his financial benefit.

A PLAYER'S OBLIGATIONS

After all, a player's contract only lasts a year, and when that regulation was made it was a big concession in his favour. But even when it expires, can he fairly claim to be free to do as he likes? In my opinion, he has still some responsibility towards his club, and he ought to study their interests as well as his own. But he is given the right to say he will not sign on again, and he cannot be compelled to do so. Surely, however, the club, too, have their rights. They may have paid a considerable sum for the player, and, if they are to lose him they are entitled to compensation. This is really what the demand for a transfer fee means in such cases.

If a player refuses to sign on, or it is decided that his services are no longer required and a transfer fee is demanded, it is possible to retain him as the club's League player without continuing to pay his wages. My own view is that if a player is retained he should be paid a living wage, under certain conditions, during the time he is disengaged. The conditions I would impose are that a man must have done his best within his ability, that he has been a good and loyal servant, and that his dismissal has only been due to the fact that he has not shown the form the club expected. If a club make a mistake in judging the value of a player it is not the latter's fault. He was no party to the sum they paid for him, and if it is suggested that they are entitled to recoup themselves at his expense I entirely disagree. If such a case were brought before the management committee, I believe they would take the same view.

But the public may be surprised to know that many demands for transfer fees are made at the request of the players. Each close season the Players' Union issue a list of their disengaged members, giving the amount of the transfer fee which has been put on them, but it is known by everyone in the game that these are only tentative sums, which are always open to variation. In innumerable instances when men have been told they were not to be re-engaged, they have been asked whether they would prefer a free transfer or whether a fee should be charged for them.

On looking back at one of the old lists, I find that an Arsenal player figured on it at a four-figure fee, and I well remember the circumstances. The player argued in this way, "If you put a small fee on me, you will depreciate my value. It would be no recommendation, and when a club comes, you can always help me to get fixed up by accepting the fee they are willing to pay." As a matter of fact, the player was transferred, and the Arsenal did not receive a penny.

With very few exceptions the players ask for a fee to be put on them, one reason for this being that there is then the possibility of their getting compensation for the time they have spent towards a benefit and which they would otherwise forfeit on leaving. Dozens of cases of this sort are within my knowledge. Clubs who have received valuable service have no wish to profit by the departure of players, and it is very common for the latter to receive the whole of the fee received for them, provided it is not more than is permitted by rule.

The rule which permits a club to retain a player and at the same time to put him on the transfer list is definitely necessary if there is to be an adequate safeguard against abuses, and I do not think there is the slightest chance of it being altered.

THE WAGE PROBLEM

But the payment of a wage to players for whom fees are required under the conditions I have suggested is quite another matter, and I feel it ought to be systematically considered. I believe the Third Division clubs are responsible for many of the troubles. When a prominent player – an old international – whose best days have passed, becomes available, they are very eager to secure him for publicity purposes, and they are ready to offer him the maximum wage of £6 a week in the closed season and £8 a week in the playing season. But at the end of the season they find that they cannot afford to pay him at this rate, and when it comes to signing on again, they propose a substantial reduction.

I have known players, engaged at the maximum rates, reduced to £3 during the summer, £5 in the playing season and £6 when they were in the team. This sort of thing causes 90 per cent of the trouble, and I believe there is only one relief from it. Third Division clubs should not be on the same level as those in the two higher grades, so far as the retention wage is concerned. It should be fixed at a lower rate. But beneficial as this would be, the change is only likely to be brought about if the Third Division clubs themselves put forward the case for it.

TRANSFER PRICES

It is said that transfer prices have fallen, and this is true, but if one begins to discuss the value of a player, it is usually put at 50 per cent higher than one ought to be expected to pay. In negotiations so much depends on circumstances. In these days it is almost impossible to keep secret the income of a club and the general financial position. Every one, too, is aware of their playing strength and their needs, and also the stability of the directors and to what extent they are likely to back an overdraft. All these things are weighed, and the price fixed is largely governed by them. Clubs may be good friends, but there is seldom anything "friendly" about a transfer transaction. They all boil down to hard bargaining, and one has to make the best terms possible.

Transfers are an interesting study. I have known of players being negotiable, as one might say, for two or three years, but no deal has been arranged, owing to the price fixed being too high. How often do clubs in such cases miss the market!

Neil Dewar, the centre forward who went from Third Lanark to Manchester United, as a case in point. In the early part of the 1931-32 season Dewar was recommended to me, and I went to Scotland to watch him and make inquiries. But the fee indirectly suggested was a fabulous one. My visit to Glasgow was generally broadcast, and I had to find a private retreat in order that I might put an end to report and rumour. But on the Saturday I went to watch Third Lanark, paying a shilling at the turnstile and standing in the open. Although Dewar scored two goals, I decided that he was not sufficiently advanced to go straight into the Arsenal side – this was before we obtained Coleman – and provide the missing link in the forward line.

In April 1932 I saw him again at Wembley, leading the Scottish attack, but the play was too fast for him. The next season I watched him against Wales, and also against the English League. In the latter match, in Manchester, he was 25 per cent quicker, both of thought and movement, and if Third Lanark had been prepared then to let him go, I think his fee might have reached even £7,000. The Scottish club, however, hung on until they were knocked out of the Cup competition, and then I presume they were compelled to transfer Dewar. I was asked if I was still interested in the player, but we did not need another centre forward. Later in the week the player went to Old Trafford, and I should imagine that the fee Third Lanark received was £2,000 or £3,000 less than would have been available a few months earlier.

SCOTTISH AND ENGLISH FOOTBALL COMPARED

I was once greatly impressed by the remark of a director of a leading Scottish club. He said, "We are only really fully extended in about one of every four matches. The remainder are easy enough to win. This is the vital difference between Scottish and English club football, and it is a very important one, in so far as it affects the development of young players." I believe this to be true, and it is on this account that English representatives have to be so very careful is assessing the value of Scottish players. It also explains why many men who are brought into English football take so long – sometimes a year – to settle down and accommodate themselves to it.

The difference in the game in the two countries, as I see it, is most noticeable in the matter of defence. English defenders are 25% more stubborn. There is more "bite" in their play, and they are harder to score against. The Scots are more given to concentrating on spectacular attacking movements. They have greater regard to style in attack than soundness in defence. In these circumstances, in "watching," say, a forward, it is essential to decide how he will fare in face of the sterner English defenders. It is inevitable that he will find the tackling faster and probably stronger and more direct. Can he make extra time for himself and still retain his form?

I am a great admirer of Scottish football, the art of the players in their positional play, the finesse and cunning with which they invest their attack. Their combined craftsmanship makes for a spectacle that is all too rare on English fields. It is not pleasant to make this confession, and I wish it was possible to so alter the conditions under which we play that we might have the same ideals and attain the Scottish standard. But, unfortunately, we are not allowed to study style. So severe is the competition, that we are compelled to sacrifice whatever ambitions we may have for effect. With us it is a case of goals and points. At times one is persuaded that nothing else matters. To get the results we have speeded up the play, and craftsmanship and ball control have, in comparison with the best Scottish style, been crowded out. Too many players are introduced into English football for their ability in tackling and defensive play generally, so that they may stop the other fellows getting the goals. We should set a higher premium on ball play and the science that goes with it; we want less of the strong-man business and more skill. English football suffers most of all at the present time owing to a lack of craftsmen.

In expressing my admiration for Scottish football, I should explain that I mean the traditional type such as the all-star team which played at Wembley in 1930 was capable of showing. Today much of the football in Scotland is poor. Indeed, I fear, since so many of the leading players have been allowed to come to this country to save the finances of the clubs, there has been a marked deterioration except in regard to one or two clubs.

MAKING ENQUIRIES

The time has come when almost every first-class footballer who falls out with his club and demands to be transferred is under suspicion. Suppose, for instance, a prominent member of the Arsenal took up this attitude, I think any club before signing him on would require to know all the circumstances. Why did he want to leave a club where every player was kindly and generously treated, where he was paid as much as the game allows, and where he ought to be satisfied? There might be an adequate reason why he wished to leave, but these are matters which I, at any rate, should want to enquire into. Indeed, one of the first enquiries I make when contemplating the engagement of a man is: "How does he behave; what sort of life does he lead?" Unless the answers are satisfactory, I do not pursue the matter further. It would not be fair to the staff to do so. Today there is only room for the decent fellow in the dressing-room. The social standing of the professional is much higher than it used to be. Most of them are well educated and intelligent, and they resent the intrusion of one who does not conduct himself properly.

SIGNING ON THE STARS

Scouting, the spotting of footballers in the rough, is a profession, or an art, in itself. Officials in my position are more accustomed to judging the finished, experienced player, and when it comes to deciding the possibilities of development in a youth, I think this can best be done by those regularly employed in the work. These are generally old professionals.

A Yorkshire friend of mine, who is a very shrewd observer, once said to me, "If I were an official of football, I should always be suspicious of the man who was easy to sign on. One might not take the view at the time, but the fellow who was hard to bargain with and who was cautious in making any change would be the one for me."

That was a new idea to me, and yet when I looked back I realised that is was a very sound one.

Indeed, I think it is true to say that all the best players are a little difficult to satisfy. This is natural. They realise the strength of their position and they are determined to make the most of it. When I signed on David Jack, the negotiations proceeded for more than a week, and even when the terms of the transfer were definitely arranged, he only decided to break up his home at Bolton and come to London after arriving at an understanding in regard to matters which affected his future.

The fuss there was over the transfer of Alex James may also be recalled. When he had decided to leave Preston, he was determined not to make any move unless it were of real benefit to him. I believe the position was much the same in the case of Alec Jackson, in his removal from Huddersfield to Chelsea.

My northern friend made another interesting observation in regard to the engagement of players "If I were the manager of a club like the Arsenal," he said, "I should like to regard every man I signed on as a potential captain, one with grit and personality." Unfortunately, these ideals are hard to satisfy – harder I think today than ever before.

MY FIRST ATTEMPT TO SIGN ON DUNNE

Every one seems to know the business of the football club. It has little or no privacy. Even matters which should be kept secret are broadcast to satisfy a curious world. It is very unfortunate.

When I left London in March 1932, in company with Sir Samuel Hill-Wood and Mr. J Edwards, the chairman and vice-chairman of the Arsenal, to negotiate with Sheffield United for the transfer of Dunne, their centre forward, I believed that only the officials of the two clubs had any knowledge of the matter. Judge my astonishment when the ticket-collector at the London station said to me as I was about to get into the train, "I hope you get him. He's a great player." When we reached the hotel in Sheffield the porter remarked, "I hope you are not going to take our Dunne away."

We met a sub-committee of the Sheffield United directors, and at eleven o'clock that night we found two pressmen waiting for us in the hotel, and they asked to interview us. Actually, we interviewed them. The information which they already possessed was astounding. I do not accuse the Sheffield club's sub-committee of telling of matters which for many obvious reasons should have been kept secret. I do not believe they were responsible for the leakage of the news. I will leave it at that.

I have been concerned with many important transfers, but never one which caused me so much annoyance as this one. Wherever I went in Sheffield I was shadowed. One night, when I had nothing to do, and realising what the game was, I took two reporters for a ride round the city. That is to say, I got into a taxi-cab and they followed me. The reporters, I realised, had their work to do, and I do not blame them for trying to get what they might regard as hot news, except on the ground that they were too persistent. But, in my opinion, they should not have known anything at all about the matter.

Fortunately, however, all the fuss and publicity which the Dunne case received had no bearing on the result, and in the end the reason for the breakdown of the negotiations was not divulged. I was able to escape from Sheffield in secret; only, I suppose, because there was no further interest in the affairs of the Arsenal.

HOW I WON A CIGAR

There is on my desk at Highbury a cigar. I smoke very little, but I shall smoke this cigar, because I feel that I deserve it. A week yesterday I left the Arsenal for the first time this season for a destination "somewhere in the north." It was suggested that I should be discovered, and that within a few hours in would be broadcast that the Arsenal were after the transfer of a certain player. There was no reason why I should not be "discovered," and so far as we were concerned it did not matter what conclusions might be drawn from my visit. They were bound to be wrong. For the fun of the thing, and as an experiment, I undertook to make the journey, attend the match, and return home without it being known that I had been away. I was well known in the place I visited, and I was very doubtful whether I could carry out my mission secretly, but I made a friendly bet of a cigar that I would succeed, and, as I have said, I am going to smoke it.

It was a wretched day and one which made me realise the comfort of a warm boardroom and a cup of tea at half-time. I need hardly say that I attempted no disguise, but I stopped the taxi-cab a hundred yards from the ground and walked the rest of the way. It was raining and bitterly cold. I paid for a seat, passing through the turnstile as an ordinary spectator, and I was sorry for the people out in the open.

My neighbour, who told me he had been a season-ticket holder for twenty years, said it was a disgrace that clubs did not cover their grounds and provide comfortable accommodation for their supporters. He offered me a cigarette at half-time, and I gave him a sweet, and we started to discuss again the covering of the grounds. We agreed that in this case the cost would be between £7,000 and £10,000, and I asked him, if he were a director, with so many calls on the Club's money, whether he would sanction the expenditure. He believed that it would be a profitable outlay.

I put the other side. Would the people be prepared to get wet going to the match even if they knew they would be protected from the rain when they arrived? He made what seemed the obvious reply. "You have risked getting wet because you knew you were going to be in the comfort of the stand."

In the train on the way home two men reviewed the results of the day, and they told me that the Arsenal had won by a goal to none. That was the second result I had heard, and I began to think that perhaps the correct one was a draw. Curiously, I was right in this surmise.

For nearly an hour they worked out how their betting coupons had fared. When we were about fifty miles from London, two other men got into the compartment with later evening papers, and, in talking with them, my original companions discovered that the betting calculations they had made were on the half time results. In the circumstances, they had to do them all over again, and when we reached London they were still busily engaged on them.

As I reflect on my adventure it seems remarkable that, though I was on a well-beaten football track all the time, I did not meet any one I knew. I do not propose to spoil the story by disclosing my whereabouts, but I may say that I might just as well have stayed at home. In the words of the scout's familiar reports – "The player would not suit the Arsenal."

THE ART OF SALESMANSHIP

A new system seems to have been adopted by some clubs in announcing that they have players for transfer. Hitherto it has been the custom to state the names of the men who would be released. Now, however, you are invited to state whom you are interested in. This does not seem to me to be a satisfactory scheme. What is the good of sending me a notice of this sort when it is perfectly plain that the players on offer are those in the reserve side? What would be the answer if I inquired about a leading member of the League side? I have not the slightest doubt that I should be told, "We are sorry, but he is not one of the players we are prepared to transfer." Of course not. Transfers of first-class players in nine cases out of ten are carried through by private negotiations, which are started by the club eager to obtain the man.

No matter how long you may be in football, you may always learn. It is evident that we have not yet reached finality in the way of arranging a transfer. One day our trainer, Tom Whittaker, was approached by the trainer of a senior club, and he was told "Our player (the name mentioned was that of an English international) is just the one you want. If you go for him, I think you can get him."

On the following day I received a message to this effect: "I am told that you are trying to get the transfer of ————. I think I can help you, and I shall be only too pleased to do so."

I wish those who plan these deals would not try to impose their "cleverness" on us. We did not want this international for the same reason that the club were prepared to transfer him.

Here is another transfer story. I was once officially informed that a club had a young player, "a second Alex James," for whom they had received so many offers that they feared they would be compelled to let him go. He was just the player for the Arsenal, and if I missed him I should be very sorry. But the matter was urgent. Four other clubs were watching him, and it was imperative that I should go at once. The fee would be substantial — £3,000. And I had never heard of the player before! Truly the credulity of the club manager is highly tested.

DISAPPOINTMENTS

In paying fees for experienced players one can easily make mistakes. I shall be surprised if there is a single official who can say that his judgement has never let him down to the extent that the results have been disappointing. The player as an individual may be all that one believed him to be, but for some reason he cannot accommodate himself to the style of play of the side. That is one, and perhaps the greatest, risk that has to be run. But

I would like to say this. One of the best bargains I ever made was the most costly one. I refer to David Jack, who will be remembered as the first £10,000 footballer, and who is worthy of this distinction.

THE £10,000 FEE

It appears to be thought that the value of the player is determined by his transfer fee. That is hopelessly wrong. His value can only be assessed by his club. A man might be worth £10,000 to the Arsenal, but his value would drop very considerably if he were to join some other club.

The £10,000 fee has not come about casually. It has been paid with the natural development of the game. Some will recall the sensation which was created when £1,000 was paid for Alf Common. At the time, it was described as downright folly, and afterwards an attempt was made to fix the maximum fee at £350. This restriction was a mistake, and my good friend, Phil Kelso, when he was manager of Woolwich Arsenal in the old Plumstead days, was one who soon found a way to "beat" it. This was when he transferred Tim Coleman with an unknown youth as a make-weight to Everton for £700. In the meantime it has been proposed to fix the maximum fee at £1,750 — I think that was the sum — but the clubs claimed the right to pay what they liked, and that is the position today.

There are two reasons why clubs strive to get the best players and are prepared to pay for them. The first is ambition and pride in doing well. The second is simply a practical business matter. They have a ground of high value, either of their own, or on lease. Thousands of pounds have been spent on it in erecting stands, making terraces, and providing all the comforts for the spectators that are possible. That is sound business, the commercialism of the showman, if you like.

If the policy is to be that of the Arsenal, what is the good of this ground if the rest of the equipment is third-rate? By this equipment I mean the team. Because of their advantages in the way of gates, the Arsenal have, perhaps, been able to move a little faster on these lines than other clubs, but I think the object in all cases is the same. The Arsenal are not the only club with high ambitions.

4

THE GAME

What Victory Implies — Converging on Goal — Helping the
Defence — Hanging on to a Lead — Opening up the Game
— Surprise — Suiting the Style to the Player — Wing-
forward Play — The Value of Long Well-placed Kicks —
The Close-passing Game — Centre Forward v Policeman —
Clever Play — Off-side Tactics — Frozen Grounds —
Captaincy — The Gulf Between Cup and League Football —
Cup Luck — Cup Worries — The Trainer — Voluntary
Helpers — If I were a Referee.

WHAT VICTORY IMPLIES

I confess that I am out to win always, and so
are the players. That is the spirit in which they go
into a match. It is laid down by law that the team
who score the most goals win, and our endeavour is
to get as many as possible. It is just as important,
therefore, that we should prevent our opponents
getting goals against us. To accomplish this, you
must be sure that the defence is sound. All this, I
know, is elementary, but it is the rock bottom of
football, and, in my judgement, you cannot get
away from it. When the Arsenal are driven on to
the defensive, it is their endeavour to keep the
middle blocked and strong, for surely it is the
danger spot. There lies the goal, and if you can

63

keep the opposition at arm's length, there is not much to fear.

CONVERGING ON GOAL

All our movements are designed and carried out on a pivotal principle. First as to the attack. We have ceased to use our wing forwards in the old style, in which they hugged the side line and centred from the corner flag. In my judgement, that is fatally out of date, though I was told not long ago of a manager who had instructed his wing men that they should aim to get within six yards of the corner flag before putting the ball over. That, I may say, is just where we like them to go, because it means that they are wasting time and allowing our defenders to get back and take up correct positions to deal with the centres. Not only is it the aim of Hulme and Bastin to come inside when the Arsenal attack, but the two wing halves do the same thing. This gives us seven men going up and converging on goal. Now as to the defence. The team swing the other way, but on the same principle. In fact, in our system we generally have eight defenders when the goal is challenged.

HELPING THE DEFENCE

In some cases, when a side are on the defensive, you see the wing men standing and waiting for the ball to come back to them. That will never do. They must at least challenge the opposing half-back. Otherwise, that player must inevitably draw a man in defence out of position, and before he can be effectively challenged he has time to place a pass accurately to a colleague. At once the situation becomes critical, if only because the player who has been drawn out of position is missing. For the player who loses the ball to make no effort to regain it is one of the commonest faults in the game. Even the most experienced players fall into it at times. It is essential, and always has been, for the wing forwards to go back and harass an opponent with the ball. They have less work to do than any other men on the field, and I have no patience with those who idly spend their time somewhere near the half-way line, waiting for a considerate colleague to give them a pass. The wing forward must work like every other member of his side, and unless he does so, he is letting them down, even though this may not be very obvious. It is, of course, even more important that the two insides should come back, and it is on this account that you get what is called the W formation. The two wing halves and inside forwards are the key men, either in attack or defence. It is certain that today — and the game has not changed as much in this respect as seems to be thought — no defence can be sound unless it has the support of the two inside forwards. An international half-back lost his place in the team a few seasons ago for no other reason than that the inside forward had not given him proper help. In match after match the poor fellow was run off his feet. What is the use of an inside forward standing up if his side are being attacked? Surely a man can do something useful to assist the fellows in the rear? Of course, we all want forwards to be in an attacking position, but before this can be gained they must get the ball. I wish spectators would appreciate this, and also that when a forward has fallen back he must have time in which to get up to join in the attack.

HANGING ON TO A LEAD

There have been many occasions when the Arsenal have won even though the opposition have had more of the game territorially. Lucky Arsenal! So it may have seemed. But there have also been games in which they have attacked persistently for long periods and lost. A notable instance of this was the match with Liverpool, in April 1933, when Liverpool scored in the early stages and then, drawing back on the defensive, kept us out for the rest of the game. This match with Liverpool was an instructive one, in showing how a team determined to keep a lead may shut every avenue to their goal.

Repeatedly Jack or James collected the ball, and was left with thirty or forty yards in which to dribble and do as he liked with the ball. The Liverpool defenders would not leave their stronghold to challenge him. They just waited for the attack to come and then covered every man who might be concerned in it.

OPENING UP THE GAME

I remember a game in which James, when standing on the half-way line, turned round and deliberately kicked the ball hard to Moss in goal. The crowd roared. They thought it was one of the Scotsman's little jokes. But James has a reason for every move. He is not given to playing to the gallery, and his long pass back to the goalkeeper was made with a view to getting his opponents out of their positions. He hoped that they would advance to meet Moss's clearing kick and so leave an opening which had previously been shut. The truth is that you can attack too long, and although I do not suggest that the Arsenal go on the defensive even for tactical purposes, I think it may be said that some of their best scoring chances have come when they have been driven back and then have broken away to strike suddenly and swiftly.

SURPRISE

I think an outstanding feature of the Arsenal's game is the endeavour to create the element of surprise. No team studies more closely the tactical side of the game, but we are always trying to get away from the conventional and stereotyped method. Our plan is to create space in which to manoeuvre, and if we can do this I have seldom any doubt about the result. Indeed, I think the openness of our attack is especially notable. We try, too, to make it rapid and direct, realising the inestimable value of time. The faster you can make ground, the more likely you are to get the opposition defenders out of position, and it is for this reason that we do not favour what is called the close-passing game. Where does that take you? Usually the ball merely travels across the field, and perhaps back again, without any advantage being gained.

SUITING THE STYLE TO THE PLAYER

It is no use borrowing ideas from another side if the style of the man is not suitable for their adoption. The Arsenal have fitted their game to the players. We have used Roberts in the best way possible; we have had the two best inside forwards in the game, and they have played to get the most out of the centre forward and two wing men. It does not matter if James never gets a goal. It does not matter who scores, as long as someone does. We depend almost entirely on team work, and this is so directed that each man may make a full contribution. I imagine that it is because the Arsenal have their own style that some of the players who are so successful in League matches are not considered for England's team.

WING-FORWARD PLAY

It is the conviction of the Arsenal that, unless the wing forward is always looking for the opportunity to go inside to seize a scoring chance, he is not playing his part properly. We are not alone, either, in taking this view, judging from the number of goals which other wing forwards obtain for their sides. I also attach great importance to the two outsides having an understanding, because it is undoubtedly true that they can make many goals for each other. The different views which are held can be traced back to the alteration of the offside law. Some authorities apparently believe that the game is just the same, or should be so, despite the fundamental change. In my opinion, football has changed from a tactical standpoint to a very large extent, and calls for new methods if the best is to be got out of the game, and if the scope in defence and attack is to be made the most of.

69

THE VALUE OF LONG, WELL-PLACED KICKS

I have been much impressed by the rapidity with which ground is now gained and the serious damage one long well-placed kick may do. There is obviously great danger when a team swarm to the attack with the half-backs following up the forwards. Should the ball be lost, back it comes, more than half the length of the field being covered by one clearing kick, and unless the necessary safeguards have been taken, it is quite likely that the two backs will be left to deal with three forwards who have almost the whole field in which to manoeuvre.

I saw Tottenham Hotspur score a goal against Wolverhampton Wanderers in something like the circumstances I have described. Whatley, a young back of great promise, made a superb kick down the middle and found Hunt. The centre forward seized the ball and had it in the net almost before the Wolverhampton defenders were prepared to deal with the situation. How different from the football of my time, when the hallmark of class was the way in which wings worked in close triangular fashion, making headway by means of six-yard passes, and taking a dozen kicks to advance as far as is often covered by two or three today. Those were supposed to be the days of science, and there was, of course, much to admire in the close work. It is possibly true that it was largely destroyed by the alteration of the offside law, which led to the introduction of new and different methods, but if the game has lost in one aspect it has gained in another. The modern style, if not quite so spectacular, undoubtedly brings quicker results, and I doubt very much whether the public would appreciate a return to the old conditions.

To go back to the match at Tottenham, one of the features of Whatley's display was his splendid sense of balance. This is one of the surest signs of the natural athlete. It is marked not only in the case of the footballer, but in the runner, the boxer, the golfer, and, I suppose, the lawn-tennis player. It was once said to me that if Jimmy Wilde were turned upside down, he would be able to remain in this position for a considerable time. In the case of many footballers, even in first-class teams, they do not know, or have not the instinct, to place their feet correctly. The foot which is, of course, important is not the one used in kicking, and it is because the other is not in the proper position to give a secure balance that the ball is often misplaced. As the game is played today, accuracy in placing the ball, especially with the long kick, is of the highest value.

Alex James declares that if one out of ten of his long passes goes right, he is satisfied, because in all probability it will lead to a goal. He is always prepared to gamble in this way. But James scarcely illustrates the point I would make. His long passes are very rarely obvious ones. Indeed, he sets the greatest store by the element of surprise, and before he actually kicks the ball, he has brought to bear his wonderful art of deception. In the circumstances, he has often to make the pass without giving himself time to take pains to be accurate.

The pass which counts for the most is the final one, and it is in regard to this that players should be especially careful. Often one sees a brilliant approach to goal and then, when it seems as if a winning shot is to be made, the whole movement is destroyed in most tantalising fashion by a careless pass which delivers the ball up to the opposition. It is easy to criticise, and I hope I do not expect too much, but the importance of this aspect of the game cannot be too strongly impressed on young players who have their spurs to win.

THE CLOSE-PASSING GAME

In these days it is very rare that one sees a combined movement in which all five forwards take part. There is little of the old close passing down the middle. I recall how the brilliant inside forwards of the Corinthians of thirty years ago used to make almost everything advance down the centre. It was only when they were in difficulties, or the way was completely blocked, that they called on their wing colleagues. But all this has changed.

The aim today is for one wing to draw the defence out of position and then make an opening for the opposite wing.

CENTRE FORWARD v POLICEMAN

One day, through the open door of the Arsenal dressing-room, I watched Jimmy Dunne pacing up and down, obviously deep in thought. His hands were pushed into his trouser pockets, his head was bowed, and his brow puckered.

"What's the trouble, Jimmy?" I asked.

"I was thinking about the match with Chelsea," he said. "As I sat on the stand (he was unable to play, owing to an injured ankle) I was sorry for George Mills. I've had some. I've played against Herbert Robert, and he keeps you so closely in his grip that you feel that you have no chance at all. I was wondering what the crowd thought about it all, and whether they had any sympathy for Mills, who is a really fine centre forward. They would if they only spent five minutes out there. And I was wondering if there was any way of beating Roberts and other centre halves who play in his style. I know all about the theory of centre-forward play, and how I should get into the open spaces, but there are none when Roberts is up against you.

Those who follow football regularly must, I think, sympathise with the modern centre forward, who is cribbed and confined as never before. But there is hope for a player who faces his problem boldly and searches earnestly for the solution. Gurney, the Sunderland centre forward, is supposed to have discovered the way to beat the "stopper" in the centre-half position, and he carries out a movement which is undoubtedly most effective. Sunderland have cultivated the practice of sending a long pass down one of the wings. Usually it is on the right flank, and it may be made by the wing half, the inside right or the outside forward. Immediately Gurney goes out to collect the ball, and the opposing centre half, whose job it is to cover him, follows. But Gurney has obtained the essential few yards start, and it is his object, as I have said, to pick up the ball and instantly swing it back into the middle. At the same time, in anticipation of this cross pass, Gallacher, the inside left, and Connor, the wing man, as well, have raced up, and in all probability whoever gets the ball has to face only one back. In the circumstances, he has a great opportunity to meet the ball on the run and deliver a telling shot first time.

This move has, of course, been fully exposed. It was practised last season, and it has produced many goals. I remember Mr. George Jobey referring to it after Derby County's first Cup tie against Sunderland, and telling how he had warned his players to be on their guard against it. But this did not prevent Gurney bringing it off successfully with the assistance of Connor. The secret of the operation is in the speed with which it is carried out. It has the effect of taking the opposing centre half out of position and leaving the middle open to a quick thrust.

Although not quite in the same way, and scarcely, perhaps, so effectively, Jack Lambert exploited it. He, too, would move out to the wing in the hope of taking the defence with him, and then, turning, try and put the ball back to Bastin. It is, too, a variation of another Arsenal plan of attack. This was when Hulme picked up a wide pass from the middle and, racing away, crossed the ball behind the centre half to give Bastin or the centre forward the chance to get in a shot. It will be seen that the object of all these schemes is to jockey the opposing centre half out of position, and if Dunne is to solve his problem I think it must be on these lines.

CLEVER PLAY

There is, I'm afraid, a good deal of confusion as to what really counts for cleverness. A back beats an opponent before clearing, and it looks splendid. But what would have happened if his trick had not come off? A half-back, swerving and dribbling with all the subtlety of an inside forward, goes right up beyond his own front line as if he may even score. Suppose he loses the ball and it comes back pell-mell, and he is out of position to assist in repelling the attack which is suddenly

75

launched against his side? Or a forward, after having beaten one man, goes on and tries to beat another, merely to satisfy his own vanity and win the cheers of the crowd, when there is nothing to be gained by the feat? You have seen it done often enough.

The trick which is merely showy should have no place in the game. It has certainly no value for match-winning purposes, and I fear it is largely from this point of view that I regard my football. It may be, perhaps, that I am too materialistic. I want the best possible football, but it must have a "kick" in it. It must be purposeful, and it must be effective.

OFF-SIDE TACTICS

Once when we were travelling together, Mr. John Lewis, who will be forever remembered for the notable part he played in developing Lancashire football, said, "The player who gets offside from a free kick ought to be made to forfeit a week's wages." This was before the alteration of the law, and it was necessary for the player to have three opponents in front of him, and not two as at present. But although the position has been simplified, the offence continues to be repeated. Sometimes I wonder whether it is always the player who is at fault, or whether the referee judges him by his position when he plays the ball, instead of when the ball was last played.

Offside tactics are creeping back. Backs in understanding with their halves are moving up to trap the opposing centre forward and wing men just as in the old days, when Bill McCracken and his colleagues of Newcastle United delighted to make the opposition look foolish. It has been called the "one-back game," but this is a mistake. To carry it out successfully, both the backs and halves must cooperate. All must advance together, and unless this plan is adhered to, it is bound to fail. I shall be sorry if there is any extension of the scheme. Clever as it may be, spectators, I am convinced, do not like it. Constant stoppages for offside are irritating. The law was altered to prevent them, and to keep the game running smoothly. Besides, it does not seem right that a player should be able to succeed by running away from the ball, for that is what offside tricks really amount to. Another objection to the system, I believe, is that it entails unnecessary risks. It may even be unsafe. Defenders undoubtedly place themselves at the mercy of the referee, and, as we know, it is very easy for him to err in his judgement of a player's exact position.

FROZEN GROUNDS

Football is a winter game, and we ought to be ready to make the best of the conditions, whatever they may be, but it is at least unfortunate when the surface makes it impossible to play in normal style. The public have no conception of the troubles and anxieties which a frozen ground causes. The boots worn on frozen ground may have short, sharp leather studs, felt bars, rubber soles, or rubber studs. When the frost is dry, rubber is good; but should the sun come out during a match, or there be any thaw, you are likely to slip about worse than ever. Rubber, too, is risky for wing men. There is usually grass down the side lines where they have to play, and on this rubber encourages a slide. In my opinion felt bars are the best. In fact, old players say that a boot with a carpet-slipper sole gives the most secure foothold. But every man must choose for himself.

CAPTAINCY

Captaincy! I agree that it is vitally important, and possibly it is a lost art. But why should a man accept the responsibilities of captaincy? In these days of fierce competition the public have no idea how difficult it is to persuade a member of a side to carry on his shoulders the cares of leading a team. No player can be played for his captaincy alone, and no team can afford to carry such a player. Besides, there are no extra wages, no bonuses, and very little kudos for a captain. Indeed, the position has duties of which many men desire to be relieved.

The captain is the mouthpiece of the staff in their relationship with the management, and he has to ventilate any grievances his colleagues may have, even though he may not agree with them. His position on the field, too, is not always an enviable one. In an exciting moment I have seen him give an instruction to a colleague and, in front of the crowd, receive a hasty and very improper retort.

How many players today have the essential personality and capacity to command? The captaincy of a first-class football team differs greatly from that of a golf club. The manager is in charge of the team all the week, with the trainer as his chief lieutenant, giving instructions as to the kind and amount of work which has to be done in individual cases. Together, they are like a small sub-committee in charge of a Test Match team offering advice to the captain. In regard to the appointment of a captain, I suggest that the best way as a rule is to leave it to the experienced players of the clubs, who are usually prepared to accept the guidance of the manager and trainer. Under these conditions, their nomination is usually accepted by the directors.

But in my judgement, the correct way to captain a side is not entirely through the appointed captain. My idea is that the whole team should share the responsibility. They should be trained to think not only for themselves but for the side generally, and they should be encouraged to make the most of the brains of every one. I shall never be too old to learn or to borrow the idea of someone else, if it is a good one. We at Highbury throw all our knowledge into a common pool, and the benefit is incalculable.

During recent years I do not think there has been a finer captain than Jimmy Seed of Sheffield Wednesday. He took charge of the team when it seemed certain that they must go down to the Second Division, and they not only survived under his inspiring leadership, but became one of the best sides we have had since the war. His men had boundless faith in him. Such, in fact, was their faith in him, that they believed that nothing could go wrong while he was on the field.

Charlie Buchan was another great captain, and I was sorry that he missed the highest honours while he was with the Arsenal. It should not be forgotten, however, that he led the side when they were runners-up for the championship, and also when they got into the Final of the Cup Competition.

Tom Wilson was a most able captain of Huddersfield in my time. Later, at his own request, he was succeeded by Clem Stephenson, who was another fine tactician. But Clem was always ready to accept the advice of Wilson, or anyone else, if it were good.

THE GULF BETWEEN CUP AND LEAGUE
FOOTBALL

The football public, I find, are puzzled by the success which has been achieved by Third Division teams in the Cup competition. From what has happened they suspect that the difference in form between the top and bottom class of the League is less than they had believed. This view may well be taken if the comparison is made by way of the knock-out match, but there is a huge gulf between Cup and League football, and many factors, which are very real even if they are not always apparent to the spectator, who has no opportunity of a peep behind the scenes, have to be taken into some account. I approach the question with some diffidence. It seems as if I shall never be allowed to forget Walsall, although the defeat of the Arsenal has several parallels in the strange and bewildering history of the competition. Besides, such a rebuff as we experienced, though bitterly disappointing, was simply one of those incidents which are bound to occur during the lifetime of a club manager.

It should be realised that a League match and a Cup tie are entirely different propositions. I do not suggest that the play in one need necessarily be different from that of the other, although it very often is. The real difference is in the attitude of the players towards the two matches. In the one everything is normal; in the other everything is exceptional. In the Cup competition, the moment the draw is made, all is excitement, anxiety and uncertainty. It does not matter a great deal who your opponent may be. All Cup ties are hard to win. Officials and players fully recognise this, and of all the surprises that are created I can safely give the assurance that few are brought about through a side underestimating the opposition. Psychological matters enter largely into Cup football. The atmosphere which is created adds enormously to the difficulties of teams. It is mainly for this reason that they are taken away before a match, so that they may be disturbed and worried as little as possible.

Now what is the attitude of a Third Division team towards First Division opponents? I imagine that few sides have ever gone into a Cup tie without believing that they had some sort of a chance. They know that the competition is made up of surprises, that almost every year some unpretentious team arise to shatter reputations. So, if there is fear, there is also hope. There is no humility about a footballer, whatever his station in Cup football. He has only to turn to the records to discover what keen, honest endeavour can accomplish, and he is inspired to make a supreme effort. It is only for one special match, and he knows that by drawing on his store of energy and showing all the courage that the situation demands he may be as effective as his opponents. There is, too, an additional incentive. If he fails, no one will think any the worse of him, whereas, if he succeeds, he will count as a hero.

So by the time the match day arrives the team have all got their sleeves rolled up, and they go out determined not only to fight to the last minute, but to show these First Division fellows, as they might put it, exactly what Cup football means. I do not blame them. From their point of view they have probably weighed the match correctly, and they have adopted the only plan by which they can succeed. They kick off with the thought uppermost: "We are not going to play these fellows as they would like to play us. If we do that, they are sure to beat us. We must make the game different from what they are accustomed to; we must try to throw them off their balance and unsettle them." There is nothing new in these tactics. They have been exploited by the smaller clubs in Cup football for as long as I can remember. There is, too, an incentive to succeed beyond the honour of victory.

The player is a stakeholder in his club, a partner who benefits indirectly from any success that may be gained. If his team has a good run in the tournament, the finances are built up and money is accumulated to meet the summer wage bill, which cripples the small clubs and is a drain on the resources of all. In these circumstances many men, when they go out to play a Cup tie, feel that they are playing for their summer wages, or at any rate, if they can bring prosperity to their club, their prospects of being re-engaged will be greatly enhanced. Is it surprising, then, that they are so keen and determined, and that they make a super effort? They play faster than in the ordinary League match, they are bolder in their tackles, and they are prepared to take more personal risks to win a prize of substantial value. They are men who have everything to gain and little to lose. The main hope of the small club is to make a good start, and the longer they keep their opponents at bay, the more formidable they become. Let them get a goal, and they pile on the pace and play harder than ever, never permitting the opposition to settle down.

The trouble is how to combat these methods when excited spectators join in to make the conditions even more difficult. If the ground is frozen, the trials of a side accustomed to play in a precise and calculated style are greatly magnified. Teams are often harshly criticised because they do not adapt their style to the conditions of the ground, or to counteract the methods of their opponents, but it is not so easy to do this as is apparently believed. This is especially true of a side who stake all on ball play and combined effort. It has never entered into their calculations to "swing it about," we may say, and even though they realise what the situation demands, it is not in them when the emergency arises to switch from one style to another. But the greatest danger which a senior team have to face is when anxiety seizes them during the course of a match. It is likely to sweep through a side like an epidemic, and if this should happen, there can be little hope that they will recover their morale and settle down to play as well as they are capable of doing.

These are the conditions which obtain when the senior club are away. Senior teams at home are never beset with the same anxieties as when away. They may lose a goal and fall behind on their own ground, but such is their confidence that they are not likely to be perturbed. This may appear strange, but it is a true statement of the position, and I think it largely explains why Third Division clubs at home are so formidable and are liable to bring about those results which, to the public, are surprises.

CUP LUCK

The only safe way to judge the chances of a team is to wait in each round for the all-important draw and the luck which it brings. To succeed, you want luck, a deal of it, not so much perhaps on the field as in the council chamber, where ties are fortuitously arranged. There are times, especially when it goes against you, when you are inclined to believe that too much luck enters into the tournament. Personally, however, I would not have the conditions altered. Indeed, to tinker with them would rob the event of much of its fascination. The best team ought to win the Cup, and despite all the fluctuating uncertainty, it usually happens that the sides who meet in the Final have gained their distinction by merit. They arrive at Wembley by their playing skill. But it is a long-drawn-out affair, and consistency of form is perhaps the chief factor of success.

CUP WORRIES

We are apt to forget that there are over 500 entrants and that the competition begins almost at the start of the season. Even for the senior League clubs, who are exempted until the third round, it extends over four months. It is a worrying time even for those who are hardened by the bitterness of the disappointments which it inevitably creates. Unless money is made from the competition, not only will the season result in a loss, but there will be no money to pay the players during the summer, and many of those who might otherwise have been retained will not be re-signed in May.

Another unhappy aspect of the competition is that interest in the club who are knocked out early is inclined to wane. This particularly applies to those, say, in the middle of the table, who are too far behind to have a chance to win the championship. There is nothing like success in the Cup competition to keep up the gates in the ordinary League matches, and I think it is also true that it is an inspiration for the players to maintain their best form.

It is sometimes said that it is a blessing in disguise when a team fighting for points, either at the top or the bottom of the table, are dismissed; that they have then a better opportunity to concentrate on their League task, but I entirely disagree. If I were in charge of a team threatened with relegation, I should regard success in the Cup competition as an aid to success in the League, always provided that we were not involved in a series of draws and left with an accumulation of postponed matches to play off hurriedly during the closing days of the season.

There is one other aspect of Cup football which I wish to mention It seems to be thought that success in the tournament means riches. This is a great mistake. As a matter of fact, there is little profit to be made unless a club gets into the Final. The First and Second Division clubs have only one blank Saturday in the season, and this is reserved for the third round ties. In the case of all the clubs who win these it means that a League fixture has to be rearranged for a mid-week date, and if it should have been played away from home the difference between a mid-week and a Saturday gate has to be made good by a system of compensation. Compensation is worked out by taking the average receipts of the three matches prior to the postponed game and the three matches subsequent to it. In these circumstances a club may actually lose money by winning a Cup tie.

THE TRAINER

In the midst of all the excitement which Cup ties create, there are men behind the scenes who in every case play a vital part, and, I am afraid, the public have a very slight appreciation of their work. I refer to the trainers, who take up their places on the side lines, ready to give any assistance a player may require. I have heard these officials described as the "bag and sponge" men. In paying a tribute to their splendid work I would go so far as to say that they are the most valuable members of every club's staff. That, at any rate, is how we regard Tom Whittaker at the Arsenal, and if trainers were transferred like players, his fee would be beyond price. I know from what I have been told that other managers place the same high value on their trainers. In recent years, with the introduction of electrical appliances in the dressing-room, their responsibilities have increased enormously. They have become almost like doctors, with no fixed hours, working into the small hours of the morning and on Sunday. They are, in fact, always on call, and it should not be forgotten that it is they who deliver the players on to the field fit and well.

We often have visitors to the Arsenal dressing-room. Several of England's cricketers were treated by Whittaker before they set out on the last Australian tour, and I may say that we are always happy to give help when possible to any games players.

It was a special satisfaction to us that Gadney, the Leicester half-back, was able to play against Ireland in the 1933 Rugby International at Twickenham. He attended the Arsenal ground just before Christmas with a badly injured ankle. One report he had received was that he would not be able to play again, and another that he would have to rest for two months. But in about a fortnight his ankle was mended, and he started to play again. I do not pretend that there was anything magical in this speedy cure. It was simply brought about by expert treatment, and I mention it to indicate what can be done to get a badly injured player fit in a short time.

VOLUNTARY HELPERS

When I came to London I had to face some difficulties which I could not have anticipated. The management of a provincial club is vastly different from one in London. Most of the troubles, it is true, were trifling, yet they were disturbing. When I joined the Arsenal, I found they had about fifty voluntary helpers, many of whom were school-masters. They came from as far as thirty miles away, and they attended all the matches at Highbury, acting as stewards and assisting in the distribution of the programmes. I knew their work to be extremely valuable and I was sorry to tread on their toes.

I think it was my second match at Highbury when I asked to meet the stewards, and I did so on the stand after the spectators had dispersed. I then learned that instructions I had given and changes which I had made in the arrangements for the games had debarred them from concessions which they had previously enjoyed. It was unfortunate, but I explained the position as I saw it, and though they did not know me, I asked them to take me on trust. I told them I was convinced they would be satisfied that the changes I had made were in the interests of the club. We still have our fifty voluntary helpers, and they continue to do most helpful work.

IF I WERE A REFEREE

If I were a referee —

Heaven forbid that I should be thrown to the lions. A manager's job is bad enough, but the critical half-bricks which are thrown at him are harmless compared with the kicks that are made at the poor fellow out in the middle with the whistle. His is truly a thankless duty, and it is ill rewarded.

But I shall try to imagine myself a referee, and set out how I would try to control a match. I know the pitfalls and the difficulties; how every decision, right or wrong, must be given instantly. Of one thing I am certain: I should stick to my guns, unless circumstances drove me to consult one of my colleagues on the line, and only when I was satisfied that I had misjudged the situation or incident would I change my decision. The referee who shows any sign of weakness is at once in a hopeless position. Players are very quick to form impressions, and so far as a referee is concerned they are usually right. And those thousands of people behind the rails will also be a very disturbing element.

The best referee is one who is inconspicuous, and I should not go onto the field with my sleeves rolled to the elbow. It is a man's job, but that is no reason why one should create the idea that it is going to be a hard one. And it is not good that one should seek to display authority by adopting an aggressive attitude. My aim would be to fit myself into the game unobtrusively, and to be heard and seen as little as possible. I should see that there was nothing unusual in my dress. I should dislike very much to wear a khaki uniform such as the Scottish referee is rigged out in. The less I blew my whistle, the better I should feel that I was playing my part.

But there would never be any doubt about my firmness and authority, and I should seize the earliest chance of showing it. The first infringement I would come down on with unmistakable strictness. It should be realised at once both by the players and the spectators that I was boss, and that I was not prepared to stand any nonsense. In that way I should win respect, because at heart players like a strict referee.

This was perhaps the secret of Jack Howcroft's popularity. As soon as he appeared on the field, the men knew that every foul would be penalised, and that they would soon be in trouble unless they obeyed the rules. They also knew that they would get every opportunity to play the game in the best sense, and that is what all footballers hope for.

From my knowledge of the inside of football I am familiar with the outlook of the player on this important question, and I am well aware that almost every referee has a reputation for good or ill. You hear men say in the dressing-room before the start of a match: "The ref today will stand no tricks." The result is that none are attempted.

Again, I would neither be dictated to nor patronised by officials or directors. I should know that if I pleased them one day, I should probably fail them the next, and instantly be held up to ridicule. I would not try to put responsibility on to a linesman. That can easily be done, but it is mean and unfair. I would avail myself of the fullest assistance my colleagues could give me, but it would be my endeavour to bring them as little as possible into the game. The jeers of the crowd would be for me.

Finally, I should be harsher in dealing with one of those sharp practices which are so petty and mean than with a charge that was too vigorous. One's sporting sense rebels against all things underhand. Let me illustrate what I mean by the view of a young professional who had recently played in his first senior match. A colleague asked him what he thought of it, expecting that he would say that he found the pace much faster, or something like that. Instead, he expressed his amazement that first-class players could stoop to such mean tricks as had been exploited at his expense by an old international who was captain of his side. He told how his jersey had been tugged from behind, in order that he should not succeed in getting to the ball, and how he had been knocked off his balance by a sly dig in the side with an elbow. "I thought they only did those sorts of things in reserve team matches," he said.

5

THE MANAGER'S BOGEY

MAINTAINING THE SIDE

Football is never free from troubles and perplexities. The sagacious schemes of management may produce a first-class side, but another baffling problem at once arises – how is the side to be maintained? Possibly it has seemed as if the affairs of the Arsenal have run with uncommon smoothness for several years, but we have had our difficulties, which have been real, though they may not have been apparent. At the time I have been conscious of how easily the team might slip back. Indeed, it is accepted as an inexorable law that a team may never create a place of security for themselves, and I have repeatedly been told that we were bound to strike a bad time. This, in fact, is the sternest task the Arsenal management have to face, and we are fully aware of the dangers and pitfalls which lie ahead.

It is sometimes suggested that a winning team are got together by luck; that men fit and blend by accident and haphazardly drop into a style which gives the best results. This has not been my experience. For any success I have achieved in team building I have had to work hard and persistently. It will, however, be insisted that I have been lucky. One has to watch a team like a thermometer, studying every varying degree of play and trying to discover the reason for it. Are men losing form because of staleness, and do they want an antidote to the daily routine of training – a game of golf, a holiday by the sea? Are they growing old and beginning to find the pace too fast for them?

If success is to continue, the cause of these troubles must be found and the remedy prescribed.

THE BAD PATCH

There is scarcely a season when some team does not crack mysteriously. There is the disturbing experience of Everton a few years ago when they went down to the Second Division with a set of players who proved themselves good enough to come back and win the championship. It is truly strange how a side fall off. It may be due to nothing more serious than a loss of swing or rhythm. But how difficult this is to recover! Players suddenly lose touch with the ball. They may even become afraid of it. I have seen men clearly hoping that no pass would be sent to them.

Twice the Arsenal have adopted what probably seemed unusual and even drastic remedies in such circumstances. Hulme showed signs of losing his form, and in order to bring him back into the heart of the game he was placed at centre half in the reserve side in a midweek match. The effect was remarkable. On another occasion Bastin lost touch with the ball, and with the same object in view he played for the reserves at inside right. He, too, was immediately brought back to his proper form.

OUTSIDE INTERESTS

There are other troublesome factors which are liable to put players off their game. I have been told that it is better that men should attend dog-racing meetings than that they should spend their free time dancing and in cinemas. I emphatically disagree. I believe that dog racing and the gambling it encourages may have a very serious influence on footballers. It may perhaps be said that I have no concern with their private lives as long as they observe all the rules of the club, but it is deeply my concern when they begin to worry about their losses, and their play is affected, as it must inevitably be in such circumstances. I knew of an international who was deposed from a First

Division side simply because he had become so involved in dog racing that football was a secondary interest to him.

Another danger is when a team or individual members of it gain some notoriety. Then one may be sure that attempts will be made to exploit them by the many friends they will have at such a time. As soon as they got into the 1932 Final the Arsenal players plunged into another life, and from a football point of view it was not a better one. Immediately the autograph hunters – what a nuisance they are – became more persistent. Invitations to dinners, theatres, and cinemas arrived, and if all had been accepted the men would never have been in their beds.

One does not like to interfere with the social life of players, and I am glad to say that it is not necessary. The men realise that in this matter there is a limit, and that they would endanger their physical condition by living too much in the high lights. As a matter of fact, a day on the golf course appeals more to them than a night of gaiety. But they must not even have too much golf. This may seem a lot of unnecessary mollycoddling, but I do not think it can be appreciated how many are the temptations which are put in the way of footballers in London, especially when they have gained the distinction of being Cup finalists, by well-meaning but mistaken people. I wish players would realise that they only count as long as they are able to retain their form on the field, and that when they fail in this, they will be left entirely to their own resources. There is not an old footballer who has not found how true this is.

I do not object to the player working. I would, in fact, encourage him to engage in some steady occupation because of the sense of security it gives him. But it must never be forgotten that professional football is a serious job demanding keen concentration, and that a man cannot succeed in it unless he is prepared to make all the sacrifices which life entails. I am afraid, too, that the publicity which the modern footballer receives is not always to his benefit. Sometimes he is given an exaggerated value and importance, and his head is turned by the praise he receives.

This is specially so in the case of the young player, who quickly believes that there is nothing more in the game for him to learn. There is no room for conceit. The game has yet to produce the complete player.

THE MODERATE COURSE

Not only are these bad patches which teams strike difficult to account for, whether they come at the beginning, the middle, or the end of a season. It is just as hard to stage a recovery. At these times directors should hide their disappointment. I know there is strong temptation to take ruthless action, but so far as the selection of the side is concerned, the moderate course is always the best.

It is during these bad times that directors become especially active and advance their views as to why this man should be dropped and why another should be put in his place. All sorts of weird reasons are put forward for failure, and equally fantastic suggestions are made for the remedy. The result is that you may have twenty different teams proposed, and under those conditions it is extremely unlikely that the best will be decided upon.

One season a team with which I am well acquainted lost their first match, and immediately they were pulled to pieces by the two accompanying directors. They started their criticism in the char-à-banc going from the ground to the station, and while they were on the platform waiting for the train they actually proposed that they should pick the team for the following match, to be played four days later.

"Don't you think, gentlemen, it would be wiser to wait until we have had something to eat?" suggested the manager. I remember that drastic changes were made in the side, and the only effect was to produce unsettlement among the men.

IMPORTANCE OF THE FIRST GOAL

At one of our dressing-room talks a player made a startling statement, and I am convinced, the more I have since considered it, that he put his finger on a major cause of much that is bewildering in the variations of team form. In effect he said: "There are two sides to the make-up of most footballers. They are great fellows when they are a goal up and they feel that they are going to win. They cannot have the ball too often. They run into position in fine style, and they shout for it on every possible occasion. But if they should lose a goal and fall behind, their enthusiasm and their eagerness for the ball go. Anyone else, in fact, can have it. It becomes like a hot brick to them, and instead of holding it they get rid of it as quickly as possible."

Are players attaching too much importance to the value of a goal and the result? In the long League season I am convinced that the team who are undisturbed by the loss of a goal, and who command the steadiness to fight back methodically, have the best chance of getting to the top of the table. I recall a conversation with an old Arsenal player who had lost his place in the side. He used to go to and from the Highbury ground with Alex James, and he told me that if he had ever the good luck to get back into the team, he would astonish me. James had convinced him that form was only a matter of confidence, and that a player went off simply because he was afraid to hold the ball and do with it what he knew to be proper.

AWAY WINS

How are championships won? I would say that they are won away from home. This reply is based on hard facts. Look where you like, I think you will find that every team in recent years who have finished at the top of the table have captured a high percentage of points on opponents' grounds. This was certainly true of Huddersfield when they gained the title in three consecutive seasons, and also of Everton and Sheffield Wednesday.

These away wins are largely a matter of confidence, of players persuading themselves that, even though the conditions may be a little strange, they are no more difficult than at home. All grounds today are first class and offer the same opportunities for good football without what may be termed local knowledge. But, unfortunately, men are affected by the change, and I have found that they are very ready to believe that referees will be more sympathetic to the home side than themselves. It may be absurd, but this idea is deep rooted, and a good deal of persuasion is required to dispel it. I long since came to the conclusion that if a side were to get to the top, they must achieve a considerable measure of success away. In fact, it is generally accepted that a draw away is equal in value to a win at home. A team who make a habit of picking up the points away must be strongly equipped for their home engagements. In a word, they acquire consistency.

CONFIDENCE

Confidence! It is the greatest asset a man can possess. Look at Gallacher of Chelsea. The Scotsman starts in every match with abounding belief in himself. Who is there to beat him? He may lose the ball once in trying to break through, but he regards that simply as an accident, and he will carry out the same movement five minutes afterwards, just as certain that he will succeed. You will see the same kind of thing in the play of Alex James. He will hold the ball, to draw and fool an opponent, and possibly lose it. But he does not decide that he must not make a similar attempt again. Rather is he the more eager to try it. He believes he can do it, and even should he fail a second time, he is not at all upset. As a further illustration of what I mean, take Herbert Sutcliffe at cricket. He may be beaten twice in an over, but he does not turn a hair. Or Wilfred Rhodes. He did not lose his length because a batsman had hit him for three consecutive 4's. He was more likely to get him with the next ball.

I am convinced that 75 per cent of players do not give half their full value because they lack confidence in themselves. They have not the courage to attempt the things which are well within their scope, and there is no doubt that spectators are largely responsible for this. The man who coined the phrase "Get rid of it" could have no idea of the harm it would cause in the game generally, but it was a very unfortunate one, and I wish it might never be heard again. Rather should every encouragement be given to players to hold the ball, for only in this way can football be orderly and methodical. Not so long ago a young player told me that when he played in the second team the ball seemed as big as a balloon, and that he could do what he liked with it. In the senior side, however, it shrank to the size of a marble.

TEMPERAMENTAL PLAYERS

What do we mean by temperament? An old Scottish golfer described it as simply common sense, and he was probably correct. But perhaps the term self-control is more expressive and better understood. I often think of the footballer as going out into the middle before a big crowd on an important occasion in much the same way as a man who has to make a speech. The one knows what he hopes to do, and the other what he intends to say, but in each case there is a very real danger of his getting hot and bothered and thrown off his balance. The trouble in regard to both of them is a mental or nervous one, and in the excitement they lose their self-control.

A footballer may be affected by the most trivial incident. He may make a mess of his first pass or shot; he may miss a tackle. Fear seizes him, and he becomes over-anxious. You see a man take the ball down brilliantly, but as soon as he reaches the penalty area, and it is time to make the final effort he does something foolish. It is, in fact, not unusual for men in these circumstances even to shut their eyes. One moment they are complete masters of themselves, and the next all their self-control has gone. It is all very strange and difficult to understand.

DAVID HALLIDAY

There are always signs of regret when a player leaves a club during a season, and especially when he is so sincerely admired as was David Halliday at Highbury. Players claim their boots as their own property, and after Halliday had wrapped up his pair to take with him to Manchester, he visited both dressing-rooms to say goodbye to his colleagues. He had, of course, spent most of his time with the reserves, or, as I prefer to call them, the spare men, and in taking his leave of them he said that he would be very disappointed if they did not win the championship of the London Combination for the fifth year in succession. The reply was to wish him a hat-trick in his first match with Manchester City.

For a player of his standing and ability Halliday had a rather unhappy experience with the Arsenal, and I may say that it was largely on this account that the directors were willing that he should leave. Naturally, he wanted to regain a place in First Division football, and we were bound to have some consideration for his interests. I have often been asked to explain why Halliday did not "come off" as it is put, with the Arsenal. I do not think it is difficult. He had not started the season with Sunderland well when he joined us, and unfortunately the form of the Arsenal was then poor. This was the real trouble. If the side has played as well as it was playing a year later, I have not the slightest doubt that Halliday would quickly have regained his confidence and settled down. Instead, he went further back, and the only thing to be done was to allow him to recover his form in the reserve side. Then it will be remembered how the team struck their best form in the Cup Ties, and, of course, there could be no change.

But long before the end of the season Halliday was himself again, as will be realised from the fact that he had over forty goals to his credit at the finish. His form was again excellent in the practice games at the start of the next season, and I frankly state that he was entitled to his place in the First team. But it was felt that we should at least begin with the side who won the Cup, and I am sure it will be appreciated that we could not possibly have moved Lambert.

ARE MANAGERS TOO SENTIMENTAL?

I remember speaking some time ago to a director who was pleased to attribute the bad time most clubs pass through to mismanagement. He told me that nearly all the trouble was due to the failure of officials to see when men were beginning to go off.

"You managers," he said, "are too trusting, so far as the old players are concerned. You even allow sentiment to influence you. A player has been with you some years, and when a doubt arises in your minds as to whether he can still pull his weight, you say, "Well, we'll give him one more season." Your sentiment is bound to land you in trouble. You are too soft. Football management must be ruthless, and unless it is, and you drop a man as soon as he begins to go back, he will let you down.

It is not easy to rebut criticism of this kind. It may be that we are too kind to the old player who has served his club well, but permanent loss of form does not come quickly, a man does not crash from first to second class in a night, and the trouble is to discern the precise moment when he should stand down. One may err one way just as well as the other. If the player does not lose his enthusiasm, his career can be extended by careful nursing, and this is a matter which is worth close study. There is one notorious case of a player who was declared by his club to be "done," and who later enjoyed the greatest triumph of his distinguished career. There is nothing a manager dislikes more than to have to tell a player that his physique is giving out, and that the game is becoming too fast for him. The man may recognise this himself, but he has the feeling that he can hold his own with the young 'uns for at least another season, and it is a painful duty to have to tell him that the game has at last beaten him. But the life of the footballer is short as well as precarious. It is a young man's game. From the point of view of safe management, the aim should be to reduce the average age of the team two or three years every season. It is, in fact, the only way, if a general break-up is to be avoided.

The "bad patch" has been a bogey to every club. Tell me one who has escaped it. Today I am afraid it is a greater danger than ever and more likely to occur, owing to the shortage of players. You may make up your mind that the key man you have relied on has reached a point in his career when – well – it is time you found his deputy. Where is he to come from? It may be that there is not the same type of player in the game. Look how Huddersfield nursed Clem Stephenson, so that they might get the last out of him. What would Tottenham Hotspur not give for another Arthur

Grimsdell, and Sheffield United for a Gillespie? Players of the outstanding ability of these men come to a club at comparatively rare intervals, and when they pass out it is almost certain that a reaction will set in.

UNDERSTUDIES

It is also unfortunate that players should grow old at the same time, and it often happens that it is not merely the case of filling one place, but three or four. That is serious but, again, it may be almost unavoidable. Oh yes, I know that we should have understudies hidden away in the reserve team and ready to jump into the shoes of the old stars who are beginning to lag. I am sorry to say, however, that you cannot work to a timetable in these matters.

My hope is that of every club manager. I want to see the Arsenal strong in every position and with each duplicated by a first-class reserve. If one could ever reach that ideal state, the future would be fairly easy. There would be the time and opportunity to build up the reserve team with young players. Even then, however, I know there would be bitter disappointments. It will never be possible for a manager to produce the reserve like a conjuror bringing a rabbit out of a hat. You might have ten, but the eleventh would be the man you wanted. This, as I see it, is the flaw in the nursery system. It cannot be depended on to produce the player when he is wanted, and he can only be obtained by means of the transfer fee. I am not against the training of young players by senior clubs. We all try to bring them on for promotion, but there are so many occasions when one cannot wait for their development, that I think the usefulness of the system is definitely limited. The position of the Arsenal certainly does not allow us to depend on it.

THE VALUE OF KEEN COMPETITION

One of the best safeguards a club can take against the deterioration of form is to have keen competition among the players for places in the side. It is not good for a man to believe, no matter how accomplished he may be, that he is sure to be picked. In that case there is a danger of his becoming slack or, at any rate, not sufficiently keyed up to make the supreme effort which modern football demands in every match. In the days when clubs were very much better off in having first-class experienced players in reserve, it was not unusual for almost every position on the field to be most competently duplicated. A man who lost his place, even through accident, could never be sure that he would get it back again, because his substitute might show even better form than he had done. If this were the case today, football all round would be the better for it. As it is, a club who have half-a-dozen first-class reserves ready to go into the side at any time are fortunate.

ADAPTABILITY

It is unfortunate that some players not only regard themselves as being suitable for only one position, but object to being moved out of it. They make a great mistake. When I went to the Arsenal, Blyth was recognised as a left-wing forward, either inside or outside. For a game against Manchester United at Old Trafford we were short of a left-half, and Blyth took the position in the emergency. For the next four seasons he scarcely played anywhere else, and his form was so good that he was rather unlucky not to get a cap for Scotland.

Adaptability should be the aim of every footballer. The man who can and is readily willing to play in more than one position doubles his value to his club. In this respect we at the Arsenal have been exceedingly fortunate. Many of the men, in fact, have played in two positions, and even three – John half-back or back, Jones outside or inside left or right half, Jack inside right or centre, Bastin inside right or left or outside left, and James in either inside position.

THE BEST AGE

It has been said that the modern game is beyond the player over the age of twenty-eight. That, of course, is ridiculous. If it were true, the outlook would be alarming, and I would earnestly plead for a return to the old offside law. Further, it would be downright folly for any man to make the game his career. Possibly the game today is harder and takes more out of the players. I think this is the case in regard to the inside forward, and it is possible that there will be a greater tendency than in the past for men who have held this position to be converted into wing half-backs. In the circumstances, what we lose on the swings we may gain on the roundabouts. The inside forward should make a good wing half, and there have, of course, been many successful conversions of this kind.

What is the footballer's best age? I believe that the average of the Newcastle side when they were at their zenith was about twenty-seven, and it is possible, despite the changes that have taken place in the game, that a man is still at his best at about this time. In few cases does a man attain maturity until he is twenty-four or twenty-five, and, provided he takes reasonable care of himself, he ought to be able to go on five or six years longer before he shows any decline. There are, of course, exceptions. We now have many boys playing in first-class football. It is a mistake, but the conditions are so stringent and the shortage of talent so acute that it is almost unavoidable. On the other hand, we have players well over thirty holding their own in remarkable fashion.

I should say the life of a footballer depends chiefly on three things, and I am tempted to put careful living first. The other two are luck in escaping serious injury, and physical build. I am always sorry for the player who puts on weight quickly, because it means that his days will be shortened. A player who once attracted me greatly said his ambition was to stop in the game as long as Billy Meredith, and, like the famous Welshman, play on the wing. Unintentionally, he told me that he was not the man I wanted. No player who sets out to scheme a long life by taking the game easily, even if he does not shirk his responsibilities, can make any appeal to a manager whose duty it is to get the best out of every member of his staff.

A photograph of the Chapman family taken in 1902 on the occasion of the Ruby Wedding celebration of Emma and John Chapman, Herbert's parents. From L-R are John, Thomas, Emma, John senior, Martha Mary, Matthew, Herbert, Henry and Ernest.

113

A portrait of Herbert Chapman taken from the Rochdale team photograph. Circa 1907.

Herbert Chapman's first portrait taken in 1881 when he was aged 3. His brothers' (L-R) John, Thomas and Matthew are behind him.

Herbert's younger brother, Henry, who won both
League Championship and F.A. Cup winners medals
with Sheffield Wednesday. He later went on to manage
Hull City.

A publicity photo of Herbert Chapman taken when he
was manager of Arsenal.

January 1934.
Well-wishers gather to pay their respects as the funeral cortege leaves Herbert Chapman's home in Hendon.

6

PROFESSIONAL FOOTBALL AS A CAREER

Necessity for First-Class Qualifications — Choice of Club — Footballers Must Work — The Possibilities — How I Met George Brown — The Minimum Age — Clifford Bastin — The Apprentice Stage — A Common Cause of Failure — The Value of Coaching — What is the End of it All — Spendthrifts — What a Man May Save — Difficulty of Making a Fresh Start.

NECESSITY FOR FIRST-CLASS QUALIFICATIONS

A boy who had just left school and who was said to have a remarkable aptitude for football was brought to me one day, and I was asked to allow him to join the Arsenal. While we were discussing the situation, the man who had brought him asked, "If you had your time over again, would you be a professional footballer?" I have since carefully considered this question, and, convinced that the life offers exceptional opportunities, I reply that I should have no hesitation in doing so. I am equally certain that I could make a success of it, but I should be a left half, and I should hope to gain some distinction in this position. It may be that I presume too much, and that my calculations are based on the belief that as a young man I should possess the knowledge and understanding which I have acquired today – that I should have an old head on young shoulders.

But in deciding to make football my life's job, circumstances would have to be taken into account. Frankly, I would prefer to remain an amateur. I do not, in fact, believe that any man would choose to be a professional if the question of his earning a living did not arise. In entering football as a professional, the one point of which I should have to make certain would be that I had the qualifications to become a first-class player. Only if one has the ability can one possibly attain the best that the game has to offer.

CHOICE OF CLUB

Satisfied that my prospects were good in this respect, the next important question would be the choice of club. I should seek one in which I should be properly coached and trained, and one that was prosperous and by its standing able to give me the full financial rewards that the laws allow.

FOOTBALLERS MUST WORK

And I should insist on one further condition. I should want to work as well as play. I say that as an old player, and I recognise the fairness of it as a manager. I am always glad when any player of mine wants to work. In the first place it is an assurance to me that the man who makes this demand has intelligence. He is thinking about the future and what his position will be when his playing days come to an end. I am happy to say that we have several players with the Arsenal who either work or who are fitting themselves to work when they must inevitably find another means of earning their living. I wish there were more. The retirement of a professional who has not a second string to his bow is one of the saddest things I know. Attractive as the possibility may be, I say emphatically that any man who enters football, and who is not prepared to work at the same time, makes a grievous mistake. Every year numbers of men go out, and their departure is a melancholy one for all concerned. No man should be satisfied with attending a ground for an hour and a half a day, preparing for a Saturday match. One who does this, and no more, has little sense of his responsibility. He has no thought for the future, and if I were now entering on a new career as a player, my uppermost thought would be – how can I safeguard my position when I have to give up?

THE POSSIBILITIES

I should want top wages and the full bonuses. I should hope to join a club prepared not only to pay me on the highest scale which the laws allow, but to give the full benefit as a reward for loyal and efficient service. Granted these things, I should believe that I was embarking on a career which offered wonderful chances.

I do not think the possibilities of a football career are fully realised. Suppose a player begins at the age of eighteen and continues until he is thirty-three. This gives him a life of fifteen years which, with ordinary good fortune, he may expect to live. He would start to earn, say, £300 a year, including bonuses, and go up to £550 or a little more. In this latter sum are included his bonuses and his benefit award, which works out at £130 a year. Under these conditions his total income from football in the fifteen years will be from £8,000 to £10,000. By what other work can this amount be earned during the same time and period of life?

They are remarkable figures, showing at once that a professional career is well worth while, if the safeguards which I have indicated are taken. Indeed, the man who has the gift of playing with the ball as an expert, should count himself extremely fortunate. It is a life, too, which provides most of the good things. As members of a club, players are given the best of everything, and they have opportunities in their tours abroad to see the world at no expense to themselves.

It may be thought that I have stressed only the best side of football, and that the opportunities which I have recounted are only for the few. This is true, but they are there for all to seize. Indeed, it is only because some men do not strive keenly enough that they do not make a fuller success of their careers.

HOW I MET GEORGE BROWN

It is a long time since I found George Brown. He lived in the mining village of Mickley, in Northumberland, and when I first met him he was only seventeen. I had seen his mother, and arranged for him to come to Huddersfield, and then I set out to find him, having been told that he had gone to the pit with a barrow to fetch some coal.

I met a lad wheeling a barrow in the village street. "Are you George Brown?" I asked. "Yes, what do you want with me?" he answered. I told him that I wanted him to come and play football for Huddersfield, and I remember how he dropped the barrow. In fact, he was so eager to be off that he would have left it in the street if I had not insisted that he should take the coals to his mother! Brown often told this story at Huddersfield, and he used to say that the day I met him was the luckiest one of his life.

THE MINIMUM AGE

Football law today says that a youth may not be a professional until he is seventeen, and I think this limit has been wisely fixed. The restriction was imposed in the interests of the boys, to curb their enthusiasm for the game and prevent them plunging into the life of the professional immediately on leaving school. The fitness of a youth for first-class football cannot, however, be determined by his birth certificate. His qualifications must be judged by his physique and temperament. Some boys are more developed physically and mentally than those two or three years older.

CLIFFORD BASTIN

Clifford Bastin signed professional forms on his seventeenth birthday, and I had no hesitation in putting him almost at once into the Arsenal side, for he was a most exceptional boy. I have never known a youth with the same stability as Bastin. Temperamentally, so far as football is concerned, he is like a block of ice, untouched by excitement. He has played in two Cup Finals, and on both occasions one might have thought he was about to take part in a match in the London Combination. Always, too, he is calm and collected on the field. Watch him run into the mouth of goal to seize a scoring chance, and you are sure that he will never fail through over-eagerness, which is the besetting fault of so many players.

THE APPRENTICE STAGE

Never, in the history of the game, was there such a golden opportunity for young players. To them I would offer this advice:

Have a definite object and ideal in training and in playing. Don't be satisfied to scrape through.

Study all the points of each player you meet, in the hope that you may learn from him, and, besides practising, get into the habit of thinking.

One is often told of the young embryonic champions who are to flash into the game and give new strength to their sides. The pity of it is that so few of them realise expectations. Unsuspected flaws in their football make-up are ruthlessly exposed in the stern match play, and they have to go back to the lower class to finish their apprenticeship. It is rare that the young footballer, no matter how talented he may be, finds a short cut to success. Not until he has been burnt in the fire can he be expected to be at his best. It is a hard, exacting life.

While we pluck the boys from their playing fields and pitch-fork them into games which are too severe a test for them, the Scottish youth is allowed to mature without his development being hurried. In this way he has the chance to learn the arts of the game under much more favourable conditions. When I engaged Alec Jackson for Huddersfield I was told that he was able to bounce the ball on his head while walking from one goal to the other, without letting it fall to the ground. I was assured that he could do that at least once out of three attempts. I never put him to the test, but I do not doubt his ability to perform the trick, for, from what I have seen, the boys of Scotland seem to spend their time playing with the ball, and any sort of ball is good enough for their purpose. Football is Scotland's national game, and every lad aspires to play for the Rangers or for Celtic. He realises, too, that to join one of these teams he must rise above the ordinary. In the circumstances, he sets out to attain a higher standard, taking this or that star as his model, and trying his utmost to achieve his cleverness.

I am convinced it would be for the good of the youths of the country if they played football in summer. On no account would I take them away from their cricket, but so many of them, both in the villages and the towns, have nothing to do after the goalposts are taken down, and I fear they only get into mischief. Besides, they would improve their play enormously by practising on a dry ground and with a light ball. But let me say at once that I have no thought of extending the season for senior football. It is long enough already, and the men

126

require a holiday, so that their flagging energies may be restored.

A COMMON CAUSE OF FAILURE

When a youth joins a club, he is pitch-forked among the older players, some of whom have probably appeared as football gods to him, but it is not long before he is disillusioned and he finds that they are merely men of clay. Instantly his outlook changes, and it is not long before he has deteriorated 100 per cent as a player, losing much of the skill he possessed. These young players should go to a club as they would to school, being kept apart from the older and experienced players. The latter have only to keep fit, and their example is not beneficial to a youth who has to learn his job. With others looking on, the youth is afraid to go out and attempt the things he should learn. He fears that he may be laughed at in his prentice state. I am convinced that it is a mistake to allow the two classes to mix.

"School" for the young players should be in the afternoon, when there is time for a coach to undertake the work of teaching thoroughly, and when no one else is looking on. If this system were adopted, I believe the chance of getting better results would be much greater. Under present conditions the proportion of young players who fulfil their promise is very disappointingly small.

Surprising as it may seem, few young players know even the rules of the game, and they never will know them. Indeed, if men had to pass an examination in them, as is necessary in the case of referees, I do not think one in twenty would pass. Every season the Football Association send to the clubs a book of rules for each registered player. I do not think that many of them are even opened. How many players, for instance, are aware of the new rule which compels a man to get the consent of the referee before he may leave the field, and which forbids his return as long as the ball is in play?

THE VALUE OF COACHING

In many respects football is not very different from the various forms of work that other men do. The player is always learning and benefiting by experience. Some are quick to absorb ideas and others slow. A Bastin may jump into the first class almost without serving any apprenticeship, whereas another may take five or six years to reach the same standard. O'Callaghan of Tottenham, was, I believe, very similar to Bastin. I remember Peter McWilliam telling me that when O'Callaghan arrived in London from Wales, at the age of sixteen or seventeen, his knowledge of the game was astonishing. Already he had mastered the art of positional play.

128

These born footballers, as we may call them, are rare, but I have found that in the case of 75 per cent of young players, not only can they be successfully coached to use the ball, but their football brain can be developed. But there must be the right approach, and also imagination in the way they are brought out. This is one of the reasons why I am such a strong believer in dressing-room discussions about the game, its tactics, and the aims to be accomplished.

WHAT IS THE END OF IT ALL?

In my days as a player football was regarded as a career with a dead end, and I remember the hard-luck stories which used to be told of the old-timers who hung about the entrance to the dressing-room on match days, hoping for help. Sometimes we meet them now. A few seasons ago, before an away match, one of these old-timers, with hair turned grey, made an appeal to us for assistance, and, has long been the custom, we had a whip round for him. Afterwards, when we were travelling home at night, the tragic plight of the old fellow was discussed, and a young player with some imagination remarked, "Is that the end? Is that what we all come to?"

I am happy to say that football, from the point of view of the player, has undergone a great change during the past thirty years. At the end of a career the future may still be uncertain, but there are many most attractive possibilities, provided a man has fitted himself to exploit them, and anyone who has to hang around dressing rooms cadging half-crowns has only himself to blame. One can have little sympathy for him. He has simply wasted his chances. Certainly football has not been responsible for his melancholy position.

SPENDTHRIFTS

There are, of course, fools in football, as in every other walk of life. What can you think of a player who as soon as he draws his benefit money proceeds to buy a motor car? I was recently told of one in London, who had been paid at the rate of £570 a year – not bad for a fellow of, say, twenty-five – and who recently had to be granted a loan in order that he might get out of the hands of the bookmakers. Another player, as famous as any in the game, once returned to his club at the beginning of the season confessing that he was broke, and asked a colleague to lend him £100. He had been living at the rate of £1,000 a year during the holiday, and he had come to the end of his tether. Only a loan could save him from selling up his home.

I never cease to tell footballers that their names will count for nothing when their lives have been spent. I feel it my duty to warn them of the position they will have to face, but I am sorry to say that many pay little heed and go their own spendthrift way. I wish I might tell of the letters I receive from players who have grown too old for the game, and who have been thrown on their own limited resources. Pathetic, even tragic, appeals are made to me to appoint them as scouts, or to find them employment as coaches. In some cases they were recently acclaimed throughout the country. They had been wonderfully popular. But now all those who professed to be their friends have departed, and they feel they are left to face a hard world alone.

WHAT A MAN MAY SAVE

The player who is determined to get the most out of football can today do really well, provided he has the skill to give him some distinction. The manager of a northern club told me recently of a member of his staff who allowed him to deduct a certain amount each week from his wages, in order that he might be sure of saving, and that he now had more than £3,000 invested. The story is true in every detail, and I think it shows the great possibilities of a football career for a man who is reasonably careful and lives a decent, straight-forward life.

DIFFICULTY OF MAKING A FRESH START

It is hard even for those who have saved their money and who set out, when their careers are finished, to make others. It is not so long ago that one who had been an exemplary professional decided to start a retail business. In not more than twelve months he lost £1,000. Another on retirement received from his club a generous benefit award of £500, and he invested the sum in a business. That, too, went at an unseemly speed.

These ventures into business, of which players can know little, probably appear foolishly reckless, but put yourself in the position of a man who has been earning £400 a year and more, who has a wife and children, and who suddenly finds himself on the list of the unemployed. The bottom has dropped out of his world. He feels that he must do something to make a fresh start and, perhaps without proper advice, he plunges into an undertaking which fails. Such a man deserves sympathy.

7

THE PUBLIC

KEEN COMPETITION AMONG LONDON CLUBS

In spite of all trade depression and the stringent economies which have to be practised, if you give the spectator what he wants and regards as value for his shilling, he will gladly pay at the turnstiles.

I agree that the clubs of London are favourably situated, but I am afraid there is a tendency to make too much of this. Repeatedly I have been told, "You can do anything; you are always sure of your gate." The truth is that, while we have a huge population to draw on, I am in no doubt whatever that unless Arsenal football is maintained at the highest standard our success as a gate-drawing club will wane. It is conveniently overlooked that we have keen competition which other clubs have not to meet. We have Tottenham Hotspur on our doorstep, and Chelsea is only a few miles away. Within the radius of about twelve miles there are eleven League clubs, and I think it will be realised that even the big football public of London is very well catered for.

We have no kick against this competition. It is all to our benefit. It keeps us on our toes, searching for new ideas and trying to provide a more attractive programme than our rivals. There is no place where it is necessary to work harder for success than London, and those clubs in the provinces who have got into the habit of pointing to unemployment figures to explain their poor gates are far too ready to seize the excuse complacently, instead of taking off their jackets and tackling the problem. The old idea that a club may sit back and wait for the crowds to come should have died long ago. In these days you have to fetch them by making an irresistible appeal, and in this respect, at least, we do not differ greatly from other entertainment promoters, in whatever line they may work.

It may be thought that I am preaching commercialism. Well, this is a side of football which has become highly important from a managerial point of view, but it should be of little or no concern to the public, and I claim that the game – the "ninety minutes," as a friend of mine describes it – is the same today as ever it was, having the same good sporting foundation and being free from all financial motives and considerations. Even the club manager and his directors, when they sit down to watch a match, forget their worrying perplexities. It is always the actual football which comes first.

Our interest in the play is no less than that of the man who pays his shilling at the turnstile, and as long as this is true I do not think there need be any fear of the game becoming engulfed in commercialism. In my view, all the developments of recent years are only a sign of progress and of the enterprising attempts which have been made to improve the game. These developments, too, must go on. If they cease, football will go back. This is inevitable. But I should be very unhappy if I thought there was the slightest danger of the playing side of the game being neglected, or of any club setting out to make and hoard money. Even the Arsenal cannot be accused of this. So far, we have put very considerably more into the game then we have taken out of it.

WHAT DO THE PUBLIC WANT?

What do the football public want? What do they like best to see? Ninety-five per cent of their interest lies in the hope that a particular team will win. There is no doubt about this, and it does not matter if the ball goes into the net off a player's eyebrow, if it counts as a goal.

When we played last at Blackburn, the referee blew his whistle soon after the start, when the ball was about three yards outside the Arsenal penalty area. "He wasn't offside," the spectators shouted, "Keep your eyes open ref." But when there had been no appeal and when everyone was mystified as to what offence had been committed, the referee gave a free kick to the Rovers, and Imrie fired the ball into the net. Instantly the crowd broke into cheers. They did not consider the merit of the goal. Blackburn Rovers were one up and on the way to winning the match. This was the thing that mattered.

This is the angle from which the spectator watches a match, and although it may be a tribute to his loyalty and enthusiasm, I think he would rather his side won badly than that they lost well. Watch, too, how the crowd eagerly await the half-time scores in other games. Listen to the talk in boardrooms. Because they are not winning as many matches as they would like, directors complain that the training is wrong: the players do not practice enough; they ought to be at it sixteen hours a day, as in other clubs. Their one concern is now to win.

DANGERS OF CRITICISM

Such is the state of football today that it is dangerous to criticise without inner knowledge. There was never a time in the history of the game when team tactics were so closely studied and such thorough preparations were made for a match. So far as the Arsenal were concerned, I made no secret of this, and I am pleased to take this opportunity to say that a man may be easily misjudged because, in the interests of the team, he plays a part which has no particular side to it, but which, according to the plans laid down, is vitally important. What are a player's orders? What is the role he has been called on to fill? Unless these matters are appreciated, and a little imagination is shown, it is quite likely that a man may be done an injustice. The fairness of the Press may never be questioned, and I do not quarrel with the views they express, but I would urge them to try to get beyond the things that are obvious before jumping to conclusions.

I would urge the public, in their view of the game, to try to appreciate the vital changes which have taken place in the tactical side during the past few years. There has been a marked tightening of defensive measures. In most cases, where old players have been appointed as team managers and trainers, systems to bring about closer covering have been introduced. In these circumstances, if a man with the ball is to evade a tackle, he is compelled to part with it hurriedly. If he holds it and loses it, he is subjected to ridicule and told to "get rid of it." Possibly it is all a matter of split seconds, but the speed which has to be exercised today does not make for accuracy of passing. In fact, it is responsible for many passes going badly astray, and probably creates the impression that the play is poor. But the next time an ill-directed pass is given, note the conditions under which it was made, and you will probably decide that the man really to blame was the one who forced it, and that it was a triumph for the defence rather than a failure in attack.

If the public could be taken into the confidence of the clubs, and allowed to know the tactics they had decided to adopt and what they hoped to accomplish by them, I think they would enjoy their matches much better. Several times I have been asked to permit visitors to be present at a players' meeting at Highbury, but we can scarcely be expected to give away our secrets. Yet a spectator may learn much for himself by closely and intelligently following the play.

In a recent match with Leicester City, Maw went over to the left wing for a throw-in, and he was followed by John, his opposing half-back. I heard a spectator exclaim, "Look at Bob John! He's out of his place again." Of course John followed Maw. To have done otherwise would have meant the Leicester man running loose without a cover, and he would at once have become an unguarded danger in an attack. To the trained footballer this is elementary, but it is such matters as this that the spectator must understand if he is to appreciate all that is best in a scientifically played game.

THE BARRACKERS

There is much unhappiness among footballers of which the public know nothing. I have sometimes thought that it would be better if they did, for it would give them a fuller understanding of many matters, and lead them to a fairer and more generous outlook on the game. For the football spectator can be, and often is, cruel.

A player from the north once told me that the crowd on his ground had been "getting at him." "I know I've not been playing well," he said. "At the start of the season the ball never seemed to run right for me, and I couldn't do right. Now I'm playing worse than ever, because I'm thinking more about the crowd than the game. They're sure to drop me, and the next thing I'll be transferred, if any one can be persuaded to take me. I'm fed up. I wish I had stuck to my job and never come into football."

I should estimate the player's worth in terms of a transfer fee at not less than £3,000, yet obviously he was perilously near the mark when he would be a dead loss to his club.

Another incident which I recall points to the incalculable harm which the barracker may do. It was signing-on time some years ago. A youth came into the office, and I put the form before him to sign. To my amazement he covered his face with his hands and burst into tears. "It's no use," he said. "I'm no use to any one in football and I had better get out. I can't stand it any longer. The crowd are always getting at me. I'm going home and I hope I shall never kick a ball again."

At the age of twenty, and after two years as a professional, he was grief stricken, and he was a player of the highest promise. I knew that he had been barracked at times, but I did not realise that he was so sensitive. Unfortunately, he had hidden his feelings, and none of us knew how he had suffered. I persuaded him to re-sign, and he came back for the new season happily enough. Moreover, for a time he got on much better. But again the crowd turned against him, and I decided that it would be better if he left and made another start, though it meant sacrificing a player who, I was convinced, had exceptional possibilities of development. The truth was that he was too sensitive.

No one expects the football crowd to be silent; we like them, in fact, to display their interest and enthusiasm. We do not object when they cheer the other side. Impartiality is good at all times. But we insist that the players should be treated fairly. We will not tolerate the noisy, vulgar barracker. I am persuaded to write of this matter not from what I have seen and heard, but from what I have been told. I have discussed it with two different sets of directors who have been troubled and perplexed by the nuisance, and I frankly stated that in my opinion, it was their duty to protect their players.

On one occasion a well-known man was persistently barracked in the Midlands, and from what I am told happened it is evident that he at last lost his temper. Turning to one conspicuously noisy spectator he shouted, "If you come round to the dressing-room at the finish, we'll settle it." Obviously, that sort of thing should not happen, and, in my opinion, if clubs gave their players proper protection, there would be little possibility of it. If the players and the public are to fall out, what is to be the result?

WHEN JACK CAME SOUTH

I remember David Jack making his first appearance for the Arsenal, in a match at Newcastle. For days he had been boomed as the £10,000 footballer, and a natural fear had seized him that, if he were judged by his display on that occasion, it would be decided that his value had been grossly exaggerated. He knew, too, that the players of the Arsenal expected a great deal from him. He had come to take the place of Charlie Buchan, and as the man who was to restore the fortunes of the club.

That match was a nightmare to Jack. He told me afterwards that he felt as if he had been thrown to the lions, and for some time afterwards he was rather unhappy, though properly proud of being the first player judged to be worth such a considerable fee. I doubt whether he has even got over it yet.

In a confidential talk I had with him shortly before the 1930 Cup Final, he told me how anxious he was that we should win, in order that the club might think that his fee had been justified. If we had lost at Wembley, my opinion would not have changed in the slightest. I should still have thought that in securing him from Bolton Wanderers I had made the best bargain of my life.

THE UNHAPPY EXPERIENCE OF JAMES

It will be recalled, too, that Alex James had an unhappy experience in the early part of the same season, and I shall always think that the dead set which was made against him was deliberately manufactured to hurt the club as well as the player. It was one of the meanest things I have ever known, and one of the finest players it has been my pleasure to see almost had his heart broken. That is not an exaggeration.

Like Jack, James was a much-boomed player when he joined us. In Scotland, where he was perhaps better known and appreciated than in England, though he had been nearly five years at Preston, he was known as "King James." He had his ideas as to how he should play, but they did not quite fit in with those we favoured, and it was necessary that he should make some change. He was always willing to do this; in fact, you could not wish for a better club man. However, before he had time to settle down to the Arsenal style, he was seriously upset by the bitter criticism to which he was subjected, and it was decided that the only thing to do was to allow him to rest.

I frankly admit, however, that I did not know how we were going to get him back into the side. It may be remembered how it was done, how he was taken to Birmingham, and brought out again in the replayed Cup tie with Birmingham. I am happy to say he has never looked back since, and that he has justified every hope and expectation. But the Arsenal nearly lost him, and if the worst had happened, those who had made the game a misery to him would have had to bear the blame.

TILTING AT THE RESERVES

There is another matter about which I would write with the utmost seriousness. This concerns the attitude of spectators towards a reserve team. It seems to be taken for granted by unthinking people that second team matches are of small account, and that they are at liberty to pass any form of criticism on the players they may choose. I assure you that to the reserves their matches are most important. They are their stepping-stones to bigger games, and when they are made to feel that their efforts are not appreciated, it is a big handicap.

I would point out further that reserve team matches are vitally important to the club. They provide the only possible opportunity for training and developing the young players who are being got ready in the belief that they will justify promotion to the senior side. We as officials give them every possible encouragement, and I would appeal to followers of the game to do the same. It is the only way, if they are to have a chance of proving themselves. We have reserves at Highbury good enough to appear in any class of football, and who can be called on to play in our most important matches at any time. That is what they are there for, and they only count as reserves because it is impossible to include all the men in the League side. In the circumstances, these players are entitled to the highest respect, and I hope it will be given to them. Those who have the welfare of the club at heart will not deny them kindly and appreciative consideration.

HOW TO STOP THE BARRACKERS

As clubs we cannot permit barracking, and the strongest possible measures to prevent it are justified. We must, as I have stated, give the players the fullest protection. They only play if in our judgement they are qualified to do so, and there must be an end to management if the crowd are to dictate the lines on which the team should be formed. Besides, in nine cases out of ten, it is a matter of opinion whether a player is a success or otherwise, and who is to decide – the responsible officials, or the crowd? Spectators, I agree, are on the whole good judges, though they are liable to be smitten with strange and extraordinary prejudices, especially in regard to individual members of a side, but it is impossible for them always to appraise correctly the value of a man's work in relation to the team as a whole, and at least in this way they are likely to fall into errors of judgement.

My remedy for barracking is a simple one. I have never had to contend with the nuisance in any serious form, but if it ever occurred, I would appeal to the fair-mindedness of the crowd, and I believe that there would be sufficient sportsmen among every gathering of spectators to see that it was stopped.

If this did not succeed, the only alternative would be strong action. A man who pays to pass through a turnstile has both rights and privileges, but he is admitted on the understanding that he behaves himself, and unless he is prepared to act as a sportsman, he should go out. I recently suggested this method of dealing with barrackers to a club who were seriously troubled by them, and I was told that they could not afford to lose their support. I further suggested that it was only because they showed this weakness that they had barrackers at all.

ORDERLINESS OF THE BRITISH CROWD

Barracking, in my experience, is never general. It only occurs in a comparatively small section of a crowd, and this makes it all the easier to deal with. Football could never have gained its wonderful popularity unless it had been strictly and efficiently controlled. Indeed, the orderliness and fine sportsmanship of the British crowd are the admiration of the world. That white horse which shepherded the people to their places when Wembley was alarmingly overrun, on the occasion of the first Cup Final, between West Ham and Bolton Wanderers at the Stadium, will remain historic in the annals of the game, and one recalls many other instances of the public's amazing behaviour under similar disturbing conditions.

THE CLUB'S RESPONSIBILITY

The governing authorities, with their duty to the public, have always insisted that the clubs should bear their responsibilities. I recall that Tottenham Hotspur were once fined £500 because the crowd were permitted to encroach on to the field of play and prevented a match with Aston Villa being carried out properly. Grounds have been shut because spectators have misbehaved, and matches which should have been played there have had to be taken elsewhere. So the clubs have a duty

146

to the game and to the public, as well as to their own players, but I am happy to say that, except in rare cases, it is not an onerous one.

A GENTLEMAN FROM YORKSHIRE

Perhaps the most awkward situation I have ever been in occurred at Highbury after a match with Middlesbrough was abandoned owing to bad light. When the referee and the players left the field, the spectators did not at first appreciate what had happened, and they did not immediately leave the ground. While they were waiting, in the expectation that the match would be resumed, the light suddenly became much better. But by this time the players were in their baths, and it was impossible to bring them out again.

When the position was realised, the crowd gathered on the field in front of the stand and shouted for me. I borrowed a megaphone and stood up in front, with the intention of informing the people that the match had been officially stopped owing to bad light.

I started: "The referee, a gentleman from Yorkshire…," but I never got any further.

A man shouted: "You come from Yorkshire, and there are no gentlemen there."

The crowd roared, and, still laughing, they left the ground, at once realising that the referee had ordered play to be abandoned; and that was the end of it.

8

THE £.S.D OF FOOTBALL

Who gets the Money? — Players are Well Paid — Expenses of a First-class Club — Uncertainty of the Revenue — The Cost of the Reserves — Young Players are a Gamble — The Young Professional is Overpaid — A Plea for More Enterprise.

WHO GETS THE MONEY?

Who is it that gets the money out of football? Apart from a few officials, 95 per cent of what is available for distribution as the rules allow goes to the players. Shareholders draw 7½ per cent as a dividend – when one can be paid – on the few pounds they have invested as their stake in the game. The reward of the directors is the right to guarantee bank overdrafts, mortgage their own personal insurance policies, and otherwise shoulder heavy financial responsibilities which they cannot really afford to undertake. All because of their enthusiasm for football.

PLAYERS ARE WELL PAID

The players think they are not well enough paid. That is an idea which we all have. Whether the game can allow them to draw more from it, the balance-sheets of the clubs tell. The Arsenal might, in their especially favourable situation, pay their players more, but they are simply members of a big combination, which is carried on by a common code of laws designed to meet the interests of all. It is not possible to set up an exception here or there. If this were permitted, the principles of control would break down utterly.

Some men may believe that their value is greater than that of other members of the side, and that they are the big box-office attraction, but they are dependent on others for their success, and they cannot be treated differently. I certainly would not like to operate any system under which financial or other distinctions were made between players in a team, except as laid down by rule.

It sometimes seems to be thought that the League is run for the benefit of the professionals. It would make for more contentment all round if it were fully realised that they are the servants of the game and of their clubs. They know the conditions, or they should do so, when they become professionals, and it is up to them to abide by them or − get out. I feel that it is necessary to write plainly on this matter. It is in the interests of the men that I should do so, because only by giving loyal service to their clubs can they hope to make the most of their opportunities.

EXPENSES OF A FIRST-CLASS CLUB

I am afraid the public have a misconception of football finance. They see the big gates and they jump to the conclusion that clubs must be fabulously rich. The cost of running a first-class club is far heavier than is realised, and to give an insight into the position, I propose to explain a few facts which, I think, will be illuminating.

First, it should be recognised that while a club can only earn money during the eight months' playing season, the expenses go on all the year round. In the circumstances, I would roughly divide the year into three periods – the seventeen weeks when the ground is closed, and the same number of weeks for matches played at home, and for those played away. Altogether, apart from Cup ties, each club has twenty-one fixtures, but the extra ones are crowded in during the early days of the season and at Christmas and Easter.

From this it will be seen that each home gate has got to cover three weeks' expenses, for, as you know, the players are paid during their holidays as well as during the season. The summer rate is, of course, on a lower scale, but when no money is coming in, the payment of the staff is a very serious drain. Indeed, it is the biggest problem that clubs have to solve. Imagine the position of a club who have finished the season with a loss and have nothing in reserve. They are driven to borrow money to pay wages, and they inevitably start the new season with a bigger debt than ever. They are compelled to reduce their expenses to the minimum, and it is largely for this reason that there are so many players out of a job during the summer.

The players' wage bill of a first-class club works out at from £200 to £230 a week. To this has to be added the match bonuses, which are at the rate of £2 for a win and £1 for a draw for each man. Then there are the trainers, the office staff, the groundsman and his assistants, and those who are engaged in searching for new players, plus their expenses in attending matches.

The expenses of running a match are also considerable. Gatemen and commissionaires cost about £25, and police an equal amount. Then there is the printing and billposting, and the entertainment of visitors, while the fees and expenses of the referee and linesmen are from £8 to £10, according to the distance they have to travel. In this way each home match of the Arsenal costs from £60 to £70. Away matches are another considerable item. In the case of the Arsenal they have only six which do not entail the team staying in a hotel one night; and, with travelling charges, the average cost of these games works out at about £50 each.

Then, of course, there are the ordinary standing charges, such as rent and rates, which may amount to as much as £1000, and the cost of the upkeep of the ground, which may vary from £2000 to £5000 a year.

Finally, there is the Entertainment Tax, which is the biggest drain of all. Roughly, it works out at a sixth of the gross takings, which means that over £160 of every £1000 taken at the turnstiles goes to the State.

UNCERTAINTY OF THE REVENUE

All these charges, it will be seen, amount to many thousands of pounds, and they have to be met out of twenty-one home games. There is the possibility of extra revenue being obtained from a Cup competition, but this is a gamble, and in budgeting for the year no club, no matter how hopeful they may be, would be justified in reckoning on this as a source of income. Again, no matter how exact and careful one may try to be in one's calculations, there is always the possibility that they may be upset by the weather. It should be remembered, too, that each match as it is played is finished, and if it should be ruined by the weather, from a public point of view there is no way of making up for it.

It has been complained of some clubs that they measure their success by the takings at the turnstiles rather than by the performances of the team on the field. From the sporting point of view this is, of course, unfortunate, but from the facts I have given I think it will be appreciated that directors are compelled to watch their revenues very closely. The only thing certain about a club's finances is the expense side of the accounts. Expenses go on piling up, whatever may happen to the matches.

THE COST OF THE RESERVES

There is, I fear, a good deal of misconception over the question of reserves. No reserve team has ever been a paying proposition, and it should be understood that the player who costs nothing is not necessarily cheap.

Let us consider the case of a youth who is signed on at the age of, say, nineteen. It can be taken for granted that he has a natural aptitude for the game, that so far as can be judged he has the qualifications to make a first-class footballer. He is engaged at £4 or £5 a week, and the club are prepared to keep him in the reserve team for two or three years. This means that they must lay out £500 or more before they can hope for any return.

YOUNG PLAYERS ARE A GAMBLE

All clubs who enter into an arrangement of this sort know that they are gambling, even though their judgement in appraising the youth's capabilities is sound. There is, first, the risk of how he will develop physically. Will some strange temperamental kink appear? Will he be smitten with that ruinous timidity which seizes so many players and reduces their value 50 per cent or more? He may, as I have said, be a fine natural player, but fail as the complete footballer, because of one of many defects which could not be discovered until he had been through the fire of stern, competitive match play. And if that should happen, bang goes all the money he has been paid in wages. That, too, is not the worst. Two or three years have been wasted in training him.

Some time ago I worked out the number of players signed on who became regular first team men, and I found the average to be only one in twelve. So much for the cheap young player. It can truly be said that not more than one out of a dozen realises expectations.

A manager once told me of a youth whom he had brought from Scotland, and who he believed would make a great player. Two years later I asked him how he was getting on. "He won't do," he said. "He's so idle that he will hardly fasten his own boot laces. I can make nothing of him, and he will have to go." The same manager told me of another hard case. The youth's talents were beyond question. He could do anything with the ball, but he had the mind of a child, and on this account he would never be fitted, he feared, to take his proper place in a man's game. As I have pointed out, these failures are costly.

I have had my own troubles in this respect. Hard as it may be to believe, I have known competent players, over whom a great deal of time and patience have been spent, lose their love for the game and resort to all sorts of tricks to avoid playing in important matches. In such cases, I am afraid, the nerve goes, and it is almost a hopeless task to try and cure the trouble. The man who shams some physical disability is not unknown, and though you may be sure that he is making a fool of you, it is hard to prove.

A few years ago I had a young player under me of whom I had very high expectations, but whenever I was on the point of promoting him to the first team, he would develop some trouble to keep him out. All the time his form with the reserve team was excellent, but finally I had reluctantly to decide that he had not the nerve for the big match, and I had to let him go. Indeed, he dropped out of the game at the age of twenty-five, although, if you had seen him in a match of little account, you would have thought him a very fine player.

THE YOUNG PROFESSIONAL IS OVERPAID

So keen is the competition for players, and so acute is the shortage, that clubs are induced to engage them at the age of sixteen, although the laws do not allow them to be signed on as professionals until they are seventeen. These boys, while they are being trained, have to be found employment, and in nearly every first-class club in the country they are to be found working on the ground. In this way they may fairly be said to earn their wages. But it seems to me that the rate of pay given to these boys will have to be regulated.

Another question which arises is, what are these boys to be paid when they become professionals? The regulations permit them to receive as much as £5 a week, and such is the demand for his services, if one should show real promise, that some club, in order to be sure of getting him, will take a risk and pay it. Indeed, if there is more than one club after a youth, there is little doubt that he will be offered the maximum.

But it does not stop there. At the end of his first season, when he may be only eighteen, and still a novice serving his apprenticeship, the law allows him to claim £6 a week all the year round; and with the star entitled to only £8 a week in the playing season and £6 a week during the summer, it will be realised how easy it is for the whole scale of pay in a club to be put out of balance. The professionals today are getting all they can expect from the game. It cannot afford to give them any more. But it seems to me that the learners are being paid excessively in comparison with those who entertain the public on Saturday afternoons. Indeed, I do not think this view can be challenged, and if ever the scale of pay is revised, it ought to be on these lines.

I agree that the value of talent cannot be judged by age or even experience. I have heard a young Arsenal player say, after having taken part in a match, "I'm told that _____ is getting £6 a week, and if that is correct I ought to receive £12." I like a youth to be impatient during his apprenticeship, because it indicates that he is ambitious to get on, and I am willing to encourage him as far as possible, but it will be seen how difficult it is under present conditions to maintain the financial balance in comparison with the older members of the club.

The young player is a new problem, which will have to be tackled. It is he who causes the wage bill to soar, and, while his cost may be a sound investment, his earning capacity for three or four years is negligible. I foresee that the matter will be difficult to adjust under a regulated system of payment, since the interests of clubs who cannot afford to adopt the maximum scale must be protected, but I do not think they would object if it were decided, for instance, what a youth of twenty, who does not win his place in the first team, may earn.

A PLEA FOR MORE ENTERPRISE

But the Arsenal were not always in a happy position, and they have only attained it by adopting a policy which, you may remember, was roundly condemned in every quarter. The directors were crazy, it was said, when they declared that it was their ambition to satisfy their enormous public by getting together a match-winning side of stars, and it was further stated that they were heading for bankruptcy when they began to pay heavily for players. No club were ever more harshly criticised. Do not forget this, because it is important in the plea I am going to make for more enterprise.

I agree, of course, that the Arsenal policy cannot be carried out by all clubs, because they have not the same public to draw upon, and there is a limit, though I do not believe it is as closely defined as is assumed, to the return they can hope to receive from any outlay. Directors say, "If we are doing well, we cannot count on bigger gates than (say) 20,000. We haven't the public to hope for more." Such a belief is a very unfortunate one. Within limits I do not believe that the drawing capacity of a team, provided it is a first-class one, can be defined. A club create their own public. I have proved this in at least two cases.

For two years Northampton had been at the bottom of the old Southern League when I went there as player-manager. "Pay me what you like," I said to the Northampton directors. The first year I

159

was in charge we finished sixth, and the next year we won the championship. We continued to do well, not only in the League but in the Cup competition. It is one of my happy memories how we went to play Newcastle United at St. James' Park, when they were at their zenith, and after drawing the first match accepted £900 to replay the tie at Newcastle. On another occasion we drew with Sheffield Wednesday at Northampton, and beat them in the replay at Sheffield. By this time Northampton football was flourishing. The gates were bigger than ever before. The team by their excellent football had created a new public.

Much the same thing has happened at Huddersfield. The Town were started in a hotbed of Rugby; the public knew little or nothing of the dribbling code. They had to be interested and won over. It was a slow and heart-breaking task, and, as will probably be remembered, the time came when it was actually proposed to move the club to Leeds, to take the place of the defunct Leeds City. The record of Huddersfield is truly a marvellous one, and, in face of what they have accomplished, no club should ever despair. Their secret, too, has always been plain for all to see. One of the most enlightened boards of directors faced the odds against them courageously and fearlessly.

Just one other instance of how shrewd management can bring about a complete transformation. In the season when Bradford City were promoted from the Third Division, Mr. Tom

Paton was the power behind the club, and it was largely through the energy which he threw into the task that promotion was achieved. During that season Bradford City's gates were almost doubled. Indeed, the interest aroused brought back memories of pre-war days when the club not only won the Cup, but were one of the leaders of the game.

We have not got to the bottom of football yet. There are still possibilities to be explored, and I think it is very unfortunate that this work is being left to a few clubs. As I see it, the trouble is that the game has developed too rapidly for many clubs. They are still old-fashioned, and are not prepared to go the pace. They are still living in what I may call the old committee state. They have not moved far enough from those days when spectators stood behind staked ropes, and an official sat in a little box and took coppers from those who entered. Under these conditions there is no chance to compete successfully with boards of directors who conduct their affairs in a progressive, business-like manner.

There is not enough enterprise in football. Insufficient regard is paid to the demands of the public. Give them what they want and you will get their support, even in these difficult times. Never mind about the experience of the Arsenal, whose success cynics declare has been built up on showmanship and publicity stunts. I think I have shown that prosperity may be enjoyed in much less favourable circumstances. At the same time, I insist that we at Highbury merit what we have accomplished. We have worked for it. It is not so many years ago that the Arsenal were simply regarded by other clubs as a chopping-block, and we could never have altered the position unless we had embarked on some new policy.

9

LOOKING AHEAD

New Ideas Wanted — Competition of the Dogs and the Speedway — The Solution: More Football — Football at Night — The Ten Yard Semicircle — Goal-Judges — Better Refereeing — Is the League System Wrong? — How to Dispel the Fear of Relegation — How to Build an England Team — Team-Building in Holland — Football on the Continent — How to Improve Amateur Football — Coaching for all Schoolboys — New Plans for the Arsenal Stadium.

NEW IDEAS WANTED

When I reflect on a new season of football it is usually with a feeling of discontent. I want something new and better to offer the public, to whom the game means so much, not only, I hope, as an entertainment, but as a sport. We want fresh ideas, and provided they are good I am prepared with the benevolent sanction of the authorities to try them out. Our great national pastime must continue to advance and develop. It must not even be stationary, because the next move would be a decline.

COMPETITION OF THE DOGS AND THE SPEEDWAY

I believe the need for enterprise to be all the greater now, owing to the keen competition of the dogs and the speedway. Dog racing! Frankly, I am afraid of it, not as a sport, though I confess that it does not make the slightest appeal to me, but because of the possibility of its association with our own game. I do not pretend to know much about it, but, as it seems to me, it is simply a medium for betting. If betting were to enter into football in anything like the same way, it would be dead in a year. I would not allow any intermingling of the two sports, and I am entirely in sympathy with Mr. Robert Campbell, the president of the Scottish F.A., in the stout stand against the tendency of clubs to play on grounds owned by greyhound-racing bodies, or even on grounds where dogs race. The footballer should be kept clear from every form of betting, and if he is to spend his days where it is openly carried out, I do not see how this is possible. It should not be thought that I oppose greyhound racing. It is entirely outside my sphere of operations, but I am convinced that it ought not to mix with football, or indeed have even a remote association with it.

The speedway is on a different footing, but it is catering for the same public as ourselves, and I think that we must meet its competition. I am afraid it is not appreciated that the young life of the country has changed very greatly during recent years. Once father and son were satisfied with a match on a Saturday, but now this one entertainment does not suffice for the week. Hence the popularity of the daring motor-cycle riders.

THE SOLUTION: MORE FOOTBALL

If this is the position, how are we to meet it? The only answer is to provide more football, and I think it can be done attractively if the lighting facilities which make it possible for the game to be played at night are utilised. The big club with its heavy standing charges requires more scope, in order to be able to increase its revenue, and others need extra receipts to pay their way. I think that this benefit can only be obtained by extending in some way the match programme, and this could be done by playing at night in midweek.

FOOTBALL AT NIGHT

I am satisfied that there is a great future for football by artificial light in England. I can see nothing to prevent its introduction, and I believe it would be a splendid success. Further, I am convinced that it is bound to come, possibly by way of friendly matches. Once launched, however, I predict that its development will be rapid.

In Brussels I saw the international team play Sparta, the match being in charge of Mr. Rudd, the English referee, and the conditions from my point of view could not have been better. That is to say, they were as bad as one could conceive. The match was played in a violent thunderstorm. So heavy was the rain, that water was gathered on the pitch. But this only meant that the white ball had to be changed more frequently. During the ninety minutes about a dozen were used. The storm did not affect one's view of the play. The field was illuminated by lights fixed to five standards running down one side behind the spectators. From each standard the rays of twenty powerful lamps were thrown across the pitch at different angles, and as they intersected and spread they did not leave a dark or even dull patch. Not once during the match did I lose sight of the ball, and it could be followed with the utmost ease. The light, in fact, was almost perfect, and as I sat and watched I wished that the public at home could always have such a good view.

I have seen games in this country when the conditions in the afternoon were nothing like as favourable. In such a light, cricket with a white ball would have been possible, and when the ball was on the ground you could see it clearly as a golf ball on a putting-green. After the match I asked the players if the glare of the lights affected their sight when the ball was in the air, and they told me that it did not trouble them as much as sunshine.

The lighting system at The Hague, where I watched a trial match, was different. In this case a standard was placed at each corner of the ground, and I was told it was thought that this arrangement gave the best results. To me, however, both fields were splendidly illuminated.

There was one other important matter which I wanted to test. It has been said that the British public would not sit in the open on a cold night, even to watch football. It was chilly both in Brussels and at The Hague. I admit that my feet were cold. But the Belgian and Dutch people followed the play with marked enthusiasm, and I believe that our own supporters would be equally attracted by matches at night. Besides, if this is the only difficulty, it can be overcome. We shall have to heat our stands. Whether we play at night or not, I think we shall do this.

THE TEN-YARD SEMICIRCLE

Three or four years ago the Arsenal wanted to borrow an idea from the Continent. On all the grounds over there a semicircle is marked round the penalty area, and the players other than a kicker of a penalty are not permitted to encroach beyond the white line.

It is an admirable arrangement, since it prevents players crowding on to the kicker and possibly putting him off his shot.

But the Arsenal were not allowed to mark their ground in this Continental style. It was not provided for in the rules. During the visit of the England team to Italy and Switzerland in May 1933, some of the members of the Selection Committee saw the arrangement for the first time, and it appealed to them as an excellent idea. One of them even declared that it was astonishing that no one at home had ever thought of introducing it. But still nothing has been done with regard to the matter.

GOAL-JUDGES

Goal-judges must come. I am convinced that referees need their help, if they are to avoid mistakes and injustices. Success in the Cup competition means so much that it is terrible that any side should go out owing to an error for which the referee cannot be held responsible. Something more should be done to eliminate the doubts which at present creep into the game, and if the objection to goal judges is on the score of expense, it cannot apply to a match which attracts fifty thousand people.

We owe it to the public that our games should be controlled with all the exactness that is possible, and I am certain that a good deal of improvement can still be made in this matter. I do not blame the referees. On the whole they play their difficult part exceedingly well, but I think that they, too, feel that they require more help. and it is only a question how this can best be given.

BETTER REFEREEING

I am keen as ever on the numbering of players. I should also like the game to be played with two referees. It is possible that dual authority might be as bad as many say would be the case; but the system is in force in hockey, and under certain conditions no harm could be done in trying it. Better control of the game is one of the biggest problems that has to be solved.

When Arsenal played St. Johnstone, in the autumn of 1932, the official in charge was Mr. Peter Craigmyle, a man of arresting personality. When he ran onto the field in his business-like style, he received a remarkable reception, and one soon appreciated the reason for his popularity.

Mr. Craigmyle's object is definitely to get on with the play, and his control was as near perfection as one can hope to see. I noted only one mistake. This was when he blew his whistle anticipating an infringement which did not occur. But from an English point of view he sounded his whistle with unusual frequency, nipping every foul in the bud, as it were, and immediately setting the game going again with the same promptness. There was no waiting. The whistle went for an

169

infringement, and the next second it went again for the free kick to be taken. Mr. Craigmyle did not insist on the play being hung up until he could take up position, as is the custom of English referees. He obviously believed that it was up to him to be ready at the same time as the players to restart the game, and he did not ask them to wait for him.

Time is one of the chief factors of the game, and it is surely a sound principle that a team who have merited a free kick should be entitled to profit by it to the fullest extent. By this I mean that they ought to be allowed to get on with the game as quickly as they choose, and not to be held up until their opponents have taken up defensive positions. It may be remembered that Mr. Tom Crew gave one of these excellent quick decisions in the Arsenal's Cup Final against Huddersfield, and that by swiftly sending a pass to Bastin, Alex James was able to score an exceedingly clever goal. They have not forgotten this incident at Huddersfield. I do not think Clem Stephenson ever will, but it was simply a case of the Arsenal playing to the whistle.

No charge that is at all vigorous is permitted in Scottish football, and it is possible that this makes for more interest and better ball play. It is undoubtedly a very thorough check on excessive keenness entering into a match. I would not abolish the fair shoulder charge, but it may be that we are too insistent that football is a man's game into which the human element should enter. Our referees are not allowed to forget this principle, and

I fear that on this account they are inclined to overlook minor offences which, in my view, should be instantly punished. We do not want too much of the whistle, but the game will never be satisfactory until the little offences are eliminated from the play, and I think referees are too indulgent in regard to the players who are responsible for them. Frankly, I like the way in which referees speed up the play in Scotland, and it may be only because of the quickness with which they whistle that they seem to whistle so much.

IS THE LEAGUE SYSTEM WRONG?

I have not the slightest doubt that the average standard of play would go up remarkably if the result were not the all-important end of matches. Fear of defeat and the loss of points eats into the confidence of the players. On the other hand, when a side score a goal it often happens that their play improves 50 per cent. What it comes to is that, when circumstances are favourable, the professionals are far more capable than may be believed, and it seems that, if we would have better football, we must find some way of minimising the importance of winning and the value of points.

For good or ill we have the system of promotion and relegation. It is believed to be the salt of the League system. I wonder whether Scotland are really satisfied since they introduced it, or whether it is thought that it has contributed to the decline which has taken place over the Border during the past few years? It does not operate too harshly in Scotland as in England, owing to the fact that comparatively few clubs ever fear the danger of losing their status.

Another effect of the up-and-down movement of clubs has been to raise transfer fees to ridiculous heights. I would go further and say that it accounts for 90 per cent of club troubles. Is it worth it? One day, probably, the question will be seriously considered. Again, it restricts clubs in the development of their young players. They are afraid to bring them in, lest the side be weakened and the confounded points lost. Only towards the end of the season, when they are in a safe position and a prize is out of reach, dare they make experiments. On the other hand, it often leads to a desperate gamble in young players, who are pitch-forked into a side who are doing badly, before they are mature enough to take their places properly. Amazingly successful as the League system has been, circumstances change, and I can foresee some of the conditions being amended.

HOW TO DISPEL THE FEAR OF RELEGATION

I once had the temerity to suggest that as many as eleven clubs should be promoted and relegated each season, and even if this went too far, it indicates how thoroughly I am in agreement with the idea that clubs should be granted greater opportunities to advance. The clubs of the Third Division have, of course, most to gain by the suggested change, and if this section of the League is ever to justify itself, it must be given encouragement.

One difficulty, as I see it, is to decide whether 25 per cent of the clubs in the Third Division are justified in wishing to be associated with the higher sections of the League, or whether their station and the limited measure of support they can command should not compel them to be satisfied to remain in a local, rather than a national, competition. But the interests of the other clubs, who are happily in the great majority, ought not to be ignored. For good or ill, they have been taken within the League fold and they should be helped. I believe, however, that all clubs and also the game would benefit if the system of promotion and relegation were enlarged. It would do something to reduce the severity of competition and make the winning of points less exacting, and I am sure that we should reach a higher standard of play.

Never a season passes without clubs being driven to spend considerable sums of money on new players as an insurance against going down. They cannot afford it, and it lands them in debt, which very probably cripples their activities for years. It may be said that, having created their own troubles, they must bear them, but really they are the victims of a system which I believe should be amended, in order to give relief on the lines I have suggested.

The anxiety which is felt in some cases when teams are threatened with the loss of their status must be almost beyond bearing. I know of one club who in their plight insisted on their players being in their homes every Friday night at nine o'clock, and officials visited them to see that this rule was observed. Recently I have heard of the complaints of players who declare that every Friday night they are spied on, and that they are threatened with all sorts of penalties if they do not observe the club curfew. I have no patience with such supervision. If I were unable to trust a player, I would not retain him. In my experience I have found that the man who is treated fairly, and in whom confidence is placed, will not let you down.

HOW TO BUILD AN ENGLAND TEAM

The idea may be startling, but I would like the English selectors to choose twenty of the most promising young players in the game and arrange for them to be brought together once a week under a selector, a coach, and a trainer. The object of this would be to enable them to go out and practice with definite schemes planned, and instead of hurrying home when the work was finished, I would have them hold a conference at which views might be frankly exchanged.

And I would keep these players together, and probably add to their number during the season. If this proposal were carried out, I think the result would be astonishing.

I may say that I have no hope of this international building policy being adopted. It will be thought to go too far, to be too revolutionary. But it is on these new lines that some of the continental football countries are working, and the value of it is reflected in the amazing strides which they have made in recent years.

TEAM BUILDING IN HOLLAND

When I was in Holland a year or two ago, I met Bob Glendinning, the old Barnsley player, who has been a coach on the Continent for several years. Formerly he was engaged by a club. Now he is in charge of the Dutch national team, and I was tremendously impressed by all that was being done to "make" players and generally to raise the standard of play.

In Holland all the potential internationals are card indexed and grouped in three classes – A, B and C. Three selectors go about the country watching these players, who have been nominated by their clubs, and a detailed report is made on their form. C is the lowest class, and if a man in this has two bad reports, he is wiped off the list. I do not suggest that a plan such as this is applicable in this country, where there are so many more players than in Holland, but the selection of the England team ought to be on more systematic lines.

Holland's international players and those who, it is hoped, will be the internationals of the future are called to headquarters once a week. Some of them have to travel sixty or more miles. They are not summoned for training. They go through different movements on the field with a view to eliminating faults. Glendinning, to all intents and purposes, is their schoolmaster, and after he has given them a lecture with blackboard demonstrations, he sets them "homework" in the form of exercises, such as how the body should be balanced in shooting or in making a centre. This homework, too, is done with amazing thoroughness by performing the exercises in front of a mirror, and a quarter of an hour is devoted to it once a day.

We could never, I fear, get the youths of this country to go to all this trouble to perfect their play. It may even be believed that football ability is inherent in the British boy, and that, owing to his own good instinct for the game, it is not necessary. But those who take this view do not fully realise the benefit of coaching.

FOOTBALL ON THE CONTINENT

Most continental sides do not yet appreciate the advantage of challenging an opponent before he can get the ball under full control. They are still shy on the tackle. In effect, they seem to say to a man, "Yes, it's your ball. Now come on and see what you can do with it." And as he advances, they retreat."

I may almost say that the continental system of defence makes attack, up to a point, easy. The point where difficulty arises is when the advance reaches the penalty area. Here the defenders are gathered together in a sort of massed formation, and the forwards are covered, or are not allowed adequate room in which to manœuvre. Continental teams, almost without exception, leave a gap in the middle and allow the opposing halves to pick up the ball as it runs loose, with thirty yards or so in which to do as they like with it.

It is in exploiting this situation that British players are apt to go wrong. They dribble up without a challenge, until, when they do pass, there is hopeless congestion in the penalty area. The English halves must not be led into the trap of dribbling the ball in the middle of the field. They must give a fast service of the ball. They must make their passes before the opposing defenders can retreat to their stronghold in the penalty area, and before their own forwards are covered. In this way, I think, the fundamental weakness of the continental defensive system will be fully exposed.

Whatever we may think of other continental nations, I am convinced that the Austrians have the ball sense which we have always believed is the inheritance of the British youth. The Austrian players are very keen students of the game, and they regard their tours as having an educative value. All of them have a great wish to speak the English language, and, unlike the Englishman abroad, they are not afraid of making mistakes in the attempt. They are equally eager to learn as footballers, and I have no doubt that they take back with them from this country many new ideas.

Defensively their scheme has changed since they first played in this country. They no longer retreat before an attack, to make a stand only when the goal area is reached. They have learned, too, to tackle and to go in and get the ball from an opponent. Indeed, they have approached much nearer the English and the Scottish style. But the centre half still goes up with the attack, with the wing halves lying out on the opposing outside forwards and further in the rear. The backs, too, are positioned to give the utmost protection to the goalkeeper. They do not, however, seem to put the same trust in the goalkeeper as is usual in this country. They do not leave him to deal with the ball when, as we should say, it is, "his." They have also a good deal to learn in covering a free kick at goal, and they do not seem to appreciate the importance of marking opponents at a corner kick. In these respects their defence is still loose.

In attack, however, their football is excellent. A succession of fast ground passes without the ball being stopped is a delight to watch, and they exploit one move which I think we might profitably adopt. Presume that the ball is sent across from the left wing. In the ordinary way, one would expect it to be collected either by the inside left or the centre forward. At the same time the opposing backs would rush in to try to intercept the ball, or make a challenge for it. But, instead, either of the Austrian forwards I have mentioned "sells the dummy" and leaves the ball for the inside or outside right, and so a great chance for a shot at once occurs.

Austrian football, as well as that throughout the Continent, is designed to please. It is none the worse for that, and those who remember the play of the Corinthian team of thirty years or so ago will, I think, see much in common in the play of the Austrians with that of the famous amateurs.

Where is this European advance leading us? I understand that a scheme for a West Europe Cup Competition on the knock-out principle is to be formulated. The idea is that the competition should comprise the champion teams of six countries, namely: England, Scotland, Germany, France, Belgium and Spain.

The proposal has much to commend it. I predict that it will be launched during the next year or two, and it will be a big advance on the holiday tours which England and Scotland have undertaken in the past. The enthusiasm for the game on the Continent is amazing, and we cannot afford to treat their enterprise with indifference or even lukewarmness, for the result of such an attitude would only be that we should be left behind in the development of the game.

HOW TO IMPROVE AMATEUR FOOTBALL

My two sons play Rugby. After a match on Saturday they return home and throw their bags into a corner. On the following Friday night they ask, "Have my football clothes been washed?" I am afraid there is little difference between the Rugby player and the Soccer amateur. Both are casual and haphazard. It is unfortunate, because I am sure that each, through his indifference to the details of his game – the little things which are really so important – fails to get the best out of it.

The amateur is association football has played a very minor part in recent years. He has, in fact, achieved little to recompense those who have devoted so much time to his interests, and the general standard of play is regrettably low. The leading clubs are yearning for players of the ability of Vivian Woodward, Kenneth Hunt, Arthur Knight, Harold Hardman, and Herbert Smith. There is a foolish idea that amateurs are too much trouble to bother about, but if one of the calibre of any of these players were to arise, he would instantly command a place in a League side.

But before there can be a real revival in amateur football, I am afraid the player will have to change his outlook and get down to the game, and play it with something of the seriousness and practical purpose which the professional is compelled to show. I shall probably be told that it is impossible to expect the amateur to give himself up to the game in the same way as the man who makes it his sole job. I do not suggest this, but it has always been my idea that, if a game is worth playing at all, it is worth playing well, and this is all that I ask. One might almost be persuaded that slackness is a virtue in amateur football. Boots are not cleaned from one week to another, and they are often of the bull-nosed type which a farmer might wear when he has to cross his ploughed fields.

Much of the training is done in a perfunctory fashion. Players do not know how to train, and they do not trouble to find out. They go on the field in the same casual spirit, without any preconceived ideas as to how they are to play as a team. Talks on tactics, discussions about their opponents! Either they cannot be bothered with them, or they consider them below their dignity: each is as good as the other man, and he is entitled to play in his own way. It is a woeful mistake, and I am convinced that it accounts in a large measure for the poor standard of play.

Teams would be astounded by their collective all-round improvement if they would only play with some settled policy, and I urge them to do this, not only because of the success it would be bound to bring, but because it would make their games so very much more enjoyable. There is too much individuality in amateur football. It is a team game, and not enough thought is given to it from this point of view. There is little study of the points which count in making for success. A goalkeeper does not think of kicking to the left when the opposite wing is the stronger one. A back kicks wildly, without attempting to place the ball to a colleague. Anywhere will do, as long as it is far enough away from his goal.

You do not hear of an amateur side discussing a mistake. Possibly it may be thought that, in doing so, some one's feelings might be hurt. But that would not occur if the discussion was on the right lines, and it was realised that the object of it was to prevent the same mistake on another occasion.

I know of no reason why amateur football should not be very considerably better. A first step to bring about improvement should be the appointment of competent coaches. Surprising as it may appear, there are players in first-class amateur football who do not even know how to kick the ball correctly.

COACHING FOR ALL SCHOOLBOYS

The schoolboys' coaching scheme inaugurated by the Corinthians and sponsored by the Arsenal has impressed me greatly. It has enormous possibilities, and unless its scope is extended, a golden opportunity will be missed. Everywhere League clubs declare "We cannot find players," and so many of the public schools have gone over to Rugby, that a very important side of the amateur game has been grievously impoverished. Here is the true explanation of the comparative decline of such clubs as the Corinthians. Their source of supply has dried up. I believe that the way back to success has been found, but if it is to be fully exploited, it must not be left to private enterprise.

The Corinthians' scheme is only the beginning of one that should be extended to cover the whole country, embracing not only the public but the elementary schools. I would go further and suggest that clubs formed by working-class youths should have the benefit of professional coaching. It can all be done, and every interest can be catered for, if there is the will and the necessary organisation is set up. The Association already have the machinery in the counties to begin the work, by holding theoretical and practical classes, which would be conducted by old players who would gratefully accept such employment. As an initial step, I suggest that the Football Association should arrange for an instructive film to be prepared and distributed all over the country. It would have great educative value, showing, perhaps more clearly than personal demonstration, many of the points of the game.

It would also be necessary to have grounds where these classes could be held. London should certainly be provided with one equipped as a football school. The F.A. have money even for this, and they could not spend it to better purpose. Such a school would be an immediate success. If players within a radius of forty miles were allowed to enter, I do not believe that one would suffice.

If the F.A. were to launch out in this way, they would also be doing work of the highest national importance, in making youths physically fit and improving their health.

Before handing the Corinthian pupils over to Tom Whittaker, the Arsenal trainer, and the coaches who were appointed to take charge of the classes, I told them of their good fortune in being the first boys to have this chance to become first-class players. I also said that, when they returned to their schools, I hoped that their coaching would be continued, and that their headmasters would invite old players to assist them to become more and more proficient.

That should be the aim, to get inside the schools and win them back to the dribbling code. I fear it may not be easy, but I feel that, unless we are prepared to offer more assistance and encouragement, Rugby will continue to make its converts. In many cases I know that we have the enthusiastic backing of the assistant masters, and we ought to retain their influence. Several masters attended the classes at Highbury, and they were as interested as the boys. The field is, of course, even vaster among the elementary schools, and here, too, help should be given. Masters with little assistance have done splendid work for many years, and it is time that this was not only recognised but practically supported.

I would like to tell briefly how the boys were instructed.

They were first taken in hand by Tom Whittaker, who explained, among other matters, the importance of kit, diet, and correct breathing. How many amateur footballers pay attention to their boots? If the studs are uneven, the balance of the player is bound to be affected. If the laces are knotted and tied at the front in a bow, it is quite likely that the ball, on being kicked with the instep, will be sliced. Most players do not put the laces through the last two or three holes, and in this way they secure more freedom for the foot than would otherwise be possible. These may be trifling details, but they are worth paying attention to, and I suspect that even experienced amateurs are unfamiliar with them.

In regard to diet, the danger of over-eating immediately before a match was stressed. Old Corinthians tell us how they used to eat steak and suet pudding with a pint of beer before a game. I am glad that we are more enlightened and know the downright folly of such a meal. All professionals today eat sparingly on match days. Some do not eat at all from breakfast until after the match, and if they did, they would be ill. Others take only a little boiled fish, and perhaps no more than a couple of pieces of dry toast.

As regards breathing, if the player does not learn to fill his lungs, he cannot hope to sustain an effort in the crisis of a match without some distress. You see players running about with their mouths open, when they should keep them closed and breathe through the nose. Football is much too hard a game, unless the player is physically fit. Indeed, unless he is in condition, he is liable to put a strain on his heart which will cause grave damage. The boys all went through breathing exercises before they went out on to the field for practical instruction. I should like to say that I do not think that a coach should have more than six players under his charge at the same time, otherwise he will scarcely be able to give the individual attention that is necessary.

The boys were shown how to kick correctly a moving and a stationary ball with both feet, how to trap it, how to take it on the chest and bring it down under control, and how to head and throw in.

That is the first stage. At the next, the position of the body in dribbling, the making of passes on the run with the inside and outside of the feet, the collecting of passes, and tackling were explained.

The final lesson was devoted to positional play and team tactics, with blackboard illustrations. At the finish the boys were given the test of half an hour in actual play, that it might be seen if they had benefited by the coaching.

Among those who were appointed to take classes were Arthur Grimsdell, the old Tottenham Hotspur captain, Joe Shaw, who will be remembered as one of the best backs the Arsenal ever had, Charles Buchan, A. W. Smith (Huddersfield), Bert White, who is now the coach at Wimbledon, and the Arsenal players, David Jack, Charlie Jones, Clifford Bastin, Frank Hill, Jack Lambert, Herbert Roberts and Eddie Hapgood. It should not be thought that this was an Arsenal affair. The scheme was initiated by the Corinthians, and the only reason I was concerned in it was that I was convinced of its excellence and soundness. I shall consider that it has failed, however, unless the Football Association can be persuaded to father coaching on a grand scale throughout the country, catering for every class of player.

NEW PLANS FOR THE ARSENAL STADIUM

A visitor who once called at the ground told me he was an architect, and produced a series of elaborate plans to make Highbury unique. His idea was to lift the playing surface eight feet, and running round underneath was to be a series of water-pipes, which would be heated to keep the turf at a certain temperature is frosty weather. Below ground would be a garage and also a store for furs. The cost of carrying out this scheme would be about £13,000, and it would produce a profit of not less than £700 a year.

"I know that it is a very trifling sum to the Arsenal," he said, "but I think it will appeal to you, because it will prevent any matches being postponed. This is my object in submitting the idea to you."

When I told him there had never been a match on the ground postponed, he was crestfallen. "Well," he replied, rolling up his plans, "a dollar would save my life."